ISBN 81-7479-004-7

Published by: Rakesh Goel, **Kaveri Books**, 125, Kadambari, 19/IX Rohini, Delhi, 110085 (India)
Phone: 7265687

Laser Typeset by: Shiki Associates, New Delhi

Printed at: Raj Offset, Delhi

PRINTED IN INDIA

Rural Marketing Administration in India

Rajagopal

1995

Kaveri Books
Delhi - 110085

Foreword

In recent years 'Rural Marketing' has gained paramount importance in promoting the rural economy. India has experienced variety of efforts through rural development programmes over the years of independence. Of these, the Integrated Rural Development Programme (IRDP) launched during 1980-81 has been considered as a major attempt at poverty alleviation which envisaged the transformation of rural economy by creating opportunities of employment and income generation for the people living below the poverty line. This programme had been bracketed with a special component of Development of Women and Children in Rural Areas (DWCRA) in 1985. Both the programmes are production-oriented and generate substantial marketable surplus in rural industries sector. Although, there had been encouraging results in achieving the physical and financial targets but the evaluation studies done in reference to these programmes often criticised the absence of marketing linkage as an important missing element.

The new policy on organising District Supplies and Marketing Societies (DSMS) worked out by the Ministry of Rural Development, Government of India in 1991, has emerged as an institutional solution to the marketing problem in rural industries sector to some extent. There is yet to arrive at a uniform pattern on organisational and functional designs of DSMS in various States. Thus, there exists different administrative arrangements for marketing of products of rural origin.

Realising the gap in the policy and practice in rural marketing and the need to evolve appropriate administrative strategy, the National Institute of Rural Development, has carried out a number of empirical studies to document the problems and prospects at micro, meso and macro levels. The analytical results have also been discussed in the seminars organised at the Institute. This book, authored by Dr. Rajagopal is an appreciable effort in this direction. He has presented case studies analysing different administrative systems prevailing for the marketing of rural products across the country. Each study highlights a different "thesis" woven around the local socio-economic conditions.

I hope the work of Dr. Rajagopal will be useful for the planners and rural development practitioners to understand the nuts and bolts of rural marketing and in formulating strategies for achieving better results in developing strong rural markets amidst the increasing competition arising out of liberalisation of our economy.

P. Vanamali
Deputy Director General
National Institute of Rural Development
Hyderabad-500 030.

Hyderabad

Preface

Rural development constitutes the core of Indian Planning and has been given a dynamic drive in all the Five Year Plans since independence. The Integrated Rural Development Programme (IRDP) evolved in the late Fifth Five Year Plan is being implemented throughout the country as a principal instrument for poverty alleviation. The IRDP incorporates numerous schemes for employment and income generation in agriculture and rural industries sector. It is largely a production oriented programme supported with the assured supply of institutional finance, infrastructure and local technology. However, many evaluation studies conducted to measure the impact of IRDP on the economic improvement of beneficiaries, have found that such a massive programme lacks in providing adequate forward linkages particularly 'marketing' to the various production oriented activities.

The rural marketing is a comprehensive subject in rural economy, more particularly associated with the rural development. It comprises broadly the primary and secondary sectors product marketing. The former sector belongs to agriculture and latter to the rural industries. The rural marketing is an integrated concept of rural economic development. Thus, it has a paramount significance in determining the rural economy by generating adequate demand and supply dynamics for the rural products in the hinterland and outside. It has been observed since long by many researchers that in all the efforts made till late eighties there was a missing link of effective market regulation and backward and forward linkages for the products of farm and non-farm origin in the rural markets. The lack of appropriate institutional support in marketing has appeared as a major setback in improving the status of rural industries. Thus, the deprived conditions of rural entrepreneurial firms have given scope for distress marketing dominated by the private merchants and led to the unorganised state of affairs.

However the government intervention in the Seventh Five Year Plan has shown a ray of light to improve the marketing conditions of rural products through the revised set-up of District Supply and Marketing Societies (DSMS) in the states. The efforts are made to understand the magnitude of the problems of rural marketing and derived some remedial policy measures suggesting new organisational set-up for the DSMS with the increased level subsidies from government.

These policies are yet to be tested pilotly in some states to draw the functional directives for implementation of the scheme more extensively. Thus in strict academic sense, there are not many studies conducted on analysing the thesis, anti-thesis and synthesis of the chronological stages of the implementing the institutional marketing system in rural areas. The literature, still seem to be obscure on many issues. Thus the attempt made in this write-up finds considerable scope to enrich the knowledge and research insights through case studies on various types of marketing systems institutionalised for rural products in different states. The case studies were conducted in Andhra Pradesh, Karnataka, Maharashtra, Gujarat and Goa states with reference to the various rural development programmes, more prominently the IRDP.

The book comprises seven chapters blended with theory and practice of marketing management. The chapter I discusses an overview of rural marketing while the chapter II discusses the administrative arrangements for rural marketing through different institutional systems. The chapter III encompasses the institutional linkages with the DSMS and individual firms. The marketing pattern of fibre products through the cooperatives is analysed in the chapter IV. Besides the case studies presented in these chapters, the book highlights the diffusion and adoption of marketing technology and the risk and threat factors in rural marketing in the chapters V and VI respectively. Over the analytical concepts of theory and practice in rural marketing the chapter VII argues the emerging challenges of rural marketing at the grass roots. The case studies discussed in this book have proved to be an effective training input in various training programmes on rural marketing organised at National Institute of Rural Development (NIRD) for the senior and middle level officials of state and central governments.

The reference period for all the case studies presented in this book is of 1991-93 and carries substantial data base on the empirical evidences. I hope this book will be useful to the administrators in the field of rural development, researchers with the interest to penetrate marketing management into the rural economy and the students of rural development to understand the complexities in institutionalising the rural marketing system. Besides, the book may largely cater to the need of the libraries as a reference document in rural economy.

I express my deep gratitude to Dr. TCA Srinivasa-ramanujan, Director General of NIRD for permitting me to undertake the case studies spread across the states. I am thankful to Dr. T Haque, Director of Centre of Agrarian Studies of NIRD for rendering valuable academic support till the completion of all studies. I also extend my sincere thanks to the investigators who were actively involved in data collection for the studies and the large number of respondents for whom it is difficult to prepare an exhaustive list, for cooperating in all respects while carrying out these case studies.

Rajagopal

Contents

List of Tables

List of Diagrams

1

Understanding Rural Marketing

Marketing is the pivot of economic development in rural areas. It is an essential component in income and employment generation in farm and non-farm sectors. The policy of rural development encompasses this premier objective in the Integrated Rural Development Programme (IRDP) which was principally formulated in the late seventies. It is a production oriented programme and marketing activity therein lies as a major component related directly with the aspect of income and employment generation. However, the implementation of the programme was started actively in 1980-81 and has been considered as one of the prominent attempts on poverty alleviation. It now operates in all development blocks in the country. The principal attempt that was made under IRDP till Sixth Five Year Plan period was to percolate credit in rural areas for the development of production sectors like agriculture, animal husbandry, poultry, fishery, industry, service and business, through set norms prescribed by the National Bank for Agriculture and Rural Development (NABARD); while no proper attention was paid for developing marketing opportunites for the production units.

In the rural development programmes much emphasis was given in creating backward linkages like credit under IRDP, training under TRYSEM, infrastructure under NREP, RLEGP and JRY; health, nutrition and women's welfare under DWCRA Programme etc. It is all one face of the coin. The main thrust of IRDP, involves distribution of loan-cum-subsidies to the target group. Merely credit mobilisation and assets creation do not attribute to real economic development of the 'target group' (those who are below poverty line). In fact, the creation of assets, under IRDP ought to have been linked with marketing activity to have a favourable implication of the programme on target group.

The Crux

There are numerous evaluation studies on IRDP conducted by government and private researchers. In the past, most of the assessments made by the government have been favourable, but the micro level studies on IRDP have not been unequivocal in supporting the official claims. Most of the studies reflected that in absence of an appropriate marketing support system for the products produced by the IRDP beneficiaries, the process of income generation is largely obstructed. In many cases it was found as the major cause of sickening the IRDP units in animal husbandry, poultry and ISB sector[1].

To overcome this problem, the Seventh Five Year Plan envisaged the need for a marketing agency to be developed as an institutional outlet for marketing of products, produced by the target group.The policy has been endorsed subsequently in the Eigth Five Year Plan document. By and large, in some states this policy was carried out and agencies with different nomenclatures were organised. They have been functioning as District Supplies and Marketing Societies/Agencies (DSMS)/(DSMA) since the beginning of seventh five year plan as an autonomous agency. However, in states like Gujarat and Goa the marketing arrangements for the products of IRDP beneficiaries have been tug-up with voluntary organisation and corporation respectively. In Gujarat, SEWA a voluntary organisation has been linked up for marketing activities where as the Goa Handicrafts, Rural and Small Scale Industries Development Corporation has been linked with Rural Development Agency for providing marketing support to IRDP beneficiaries.

The Kerala Rural Development and Marketing Society (KERAMS) has been organised in the state in 1986 as an 'apex' society with its branches in districts. Of late, considerable stress has been given by the Union Government in formulating a policy for providing input supply and marketing assistance at state level and has been emphasised in the Seventh Five Year Plan. The major problem in carrying out the implications of the policy has been due to miss-matches production and marketing linkages. It is found that decision for providing marketing support at the time of grounding the unit is not taken which generates marketing gap. Why such decisions are not taken at the time of grounding schemes and what makes it difficult are the debatable issues. Since marketing is one of the prerequisites for income generation but in the absence of proper market linkages in IRDP, whether a beneficiary lying below poverty line is 'net benefited'? The question calls for an indepth enquiry into the matter.

The Plan documents envisaged the need for marketing facilities in rural areas. The plan stated that as regards the economic viability of the household enterprises, the major handicaps experienced are pertaining to the supply of raw materials, access to credit and facilities for marketing. As a result there is considerable exploitation of these households by the middlemen. Further, the document adds that the government sponsored programmes for the poor, such as dairy and poultry, account for only a small proportion of total market for such products now, sometimes even less than one per cent[2].

Myth and Reality

It is pointed out in the plan document that the major areas of weakness under IRDP are the absence of infrastructural support, backward and forward linkages. In order to ensure the requirement of programme specific and general infrastructure at local level, funds were provided separately, over and above the subsidy funds, as a part of the overall outlay under IRDP. These funds, among other things were earmarked for utilisation in developing institutions such as 'District Supplies and Marketing Societies' (DSMS) at district level to take care of raw materials, input requirements and out put marketing. It is further envisaged that an infrastructure sub-plan should be prepared as an integral part of the sub-sectoral district plans.

During the Seventh Five Year Plan period, the concept of DSMS was not taken-up with zest by all the state governments. Consequently, such an institution for marketing support emerged only in few states. Of these, Kerala made a headway by organising such society at 'Apex' level as Kerala Rural Development and Marketing Society (KERAMS) with its branches at district level. It may also be noted that a similar kind of approach was followed in Sixth plan period as 'Single Window System' at district level but it had a major criticism, of absence of marketing facilities for majority of commodities produced in various sectors.

In recent development an integrated system of backward and forward linkages have been established in Karnataka to support the economic reformation of rural artisans in true sense. The VISWA programme designed and implemented by the Karnataka government sets a clear distinction between the myth and reality of rural economic development by generating additional employment and income at the grass roots. The system involves the sectoral corporations and boards for providing input supply, training, finance and marketing support to the beneficiaries. It is in this background the government of Karnataka has attempted to implement a continuous rural productive employment programme in the fall of 1990.

The existing structure of DSMS caters to the marketing needs of limited commodities. Due to various organisational constraints it is unable to expand the marketing activities for majority of the commodities produced by the target group beneficiaries assisted under various programmes in the district. The major problems experienced by the officers in making their unit viable are in relation to the availability of supporting services and infrastructural facilities like, marketing, input availability, repair and maintenance facilities, worksheds etc.

Administrative responsiveness to the implementation process of rural development programmes is one of the major considerations for effective commissioning of the programme or scheme thereof. By and large it is a process of inter and intra-departmental co-ordination at various levels. The basic requirement is the co-ordination between two economic segments of production and marketing. The process of implementation of various development programmes in rural areas throughout the Five Year Plans have been experienced that most of them are production oriented. Thus in the operational process of the programme, the concept of marketing is over looked though it is one of the important forward linkages for production promotion, income generation and overall economic growth of the sector. Therefore, the greater economic crisis has been often emphasised for market responsiveness of rural products[3]. In this regard, there is a need for, greater concentration on state protection at embryonic stage of rural industries, technology transfer and development of infrastructure. However, in agriculture sector, regulating the trade in village markets need to be given due importance.

Some Experiments

In the recent past many approaches have been experimented on pilot basis to provide better post-credit facilities to the entrepreneurs engaged in different trades assisted under various rural development programmes. The various studies on evaluation and critical appraisal of different rural development programmes like IRDP, DWCRA etc have pointed out the inadequate linkages as wide gulf between the policy and programme implementation stages. The efforts for providing effective backward linkages consisting of credit, extension services and infrastructure is concrescent since the inception of the programmes. However, the forward linkage mainly comprising MARKETING function remained at lower priority all through the Sixth and Seventh Five Year Plans.The policy of organising the District Supply and Marketing Society [DSMS] as an agency for input supply, marketing assistance, credit regulation and business promotion had been the state subject and did not receive high attention till the late nineties. Of late, the need for making brisk marketing efforts for the products of rural industries, service and business sector was found alarmingly for integrating the overall economic activity of income generation at an anticipated rate.

In Andhra Pradesh, Karnataka, Tamilnadu, Kerala, Gujarat and Goa such experiments have been carried out in some districts establishing an institutional linkage to serve as a facilitator for enrouting the products in the open market and regulating the credit provided to the beneficiaries[4]. These institutions are organised on the lines of DSMS and function as an integrated part of District Rural Development Agencies, corporations and voluntary organisations. They are autonomous bodies catering the input supply and marketing assistance to the beneficiaries assisted under IRDP and DWCRA programmes. The administrative arrangements for providing the linkages through these institutes is also not uniformal in many states.

The linkages established with the sectoral corporations and the boards for VISHWA beneficiaries in Karnataka and DIC, the coordinating and monitoring agency have two different ethos. The corporations and boards are the profit making organisations and incorporated as a public sector undertaking under companies Act. On the contrary DIC is an agency functioning for the development of rural industries on behalf of the government. However both the functionaries have been linked in one of the common motos of serving non-farm sector by facilitating input requirements and output marketing. The advantage of the sectoral marketing agencies is that they have profit oriented goals which help in devicing better marketing strategies for the VISHWA products also at par with their indigenous products in the market. This provides a break for the products of rural entreprises to sustain the market practices and gain consumer recognition.

The linkages for the beneficiaries of IRDP in the state are established by the KVIB and in particular it caters to the leather industry in the Kolhapur district. The Government of Maharashtra has provided a revolving capital of Rs 4.76 lakhs during 1992-92 to the Board to meet the input requirement of the beneficiaries and assist in their product marketing. The Board is working on very formal administrative dynamics which does not make it mandatory neither for the Board to procure the finished product from the beneficiaries nor to the beneficiaries to sell their produce to the Board. However, the Board has provided raw materials worth Rs 2.86 lakhs during 1992-93 to 10 beneficiaries. The board procures the finished goods from all the IRDP beneficiaries provided they are of prescribed standard. In strict sense the administrative arrangement made for input supply and marketing assistance in the state does not integrate both the activities with the link institution. The KVIB largely stands as an alternative channel for the artisans in the open market but in no sense this channel integrates the input supply and output marketing activity for the IRDP beneficiaries like VISHWA programme in Karnataka. In all, the KVIB provides the raw material to the rural artisan units of DRDA as a continuous process provided the artisans demand for getting the same from the KVIB channel.

The DWCRA beneficiaries of Banaskantha district of

Gujarat have been receiving the logistic support in marketing their products through the intervention of SEWA. The linkages are established assessing the need of the beneficaries to set in the activity to manufacture the products in tune to the market demand.

The environmental mapping is one of the principal exercises done for organising any product marketing group in the hinterland. The assessment of physical and financial resources required for production and distribution of products, incremental income and the customer needs are the important issues which are considered in mapping the market economy as a pre-requisite. The inputs and approaches for this analysis are the opinion surveys and the leadership survey. The leadership survey consists of content analysis of observation from two distinct sources — product leader and price leader in the market.

It is observed that the institutional linkages for the beneficiaries of rural development programmes has not only helped them in getting the quality inputs on time at reasonable price and assured marketing for their products but also helped in developing business logistics and inclination towards technology adoption. It has been inculcated by the link institution in the beneficiaries through extensive training support and informal work participation. It is observed that the rate of product drop-outs prior to the institutional linkages were as high as 15.73 per cent of the total value of the gross production in footware and leather goods which is reduced to 4.19 per cent following the institutional intervention in marketing. In case of mat-weaving the drop outs were higher to the extent of 19.36 per cent before the mat weavers covered under the VISHWA programme. The quality control, skill upgradation and mechanisation has helped in reviving the products in the open market. The patch-work and weaving in Banaskantha district had also faced such problems to the extent of 11.63 per cent during 1988-90. Later the establishment of SEWA link with the women entrepreneurs has provided manifold opportunities for the product in the market. The success of such organised efforts lies in various behavioural and technical skills like effective leadership, participatory management, development market review [DMR], skill upgradation and technology adoption. Such exercise reduced the rate of product drop out from the market to a minimum of 2.06 per cent, which is mostly occupied by the last quality stocks. However, the there were no product drop-outs in the continuing institutional linkage system in the selected trades.

Problems Foreseen

The revised scheme of DSMS envisages as many as 22 broad functions which mainly include assuming fifty per cent of market for the cottage and rural industries products, developing required market infrastructure, liaisoning with government departments and public sector undertakings grading the rural products etc. The revised estimates provide an outlay of Rs. 10 lakhs per DSMS with a seed capital to procure products up to Rs. 5 lakh. However the basic question that arises is what is structure of organisation? Yet there is no pattern appeared uniformal for DSMS.

The four options to organise the DSMS can be thought of in detail. They are DSMS as (i) a co-operative society of IRDP beneficiaries (ii) a charitable society (iii) a voluntary organisation and (iv) an integrated part of the existing DRDA. However, the first two options, namely organising DSMS as a co-operative and charitable society may not be agreeable as a blanket approach because of various administrative and financial problem, in different states.

The view of organising the DSMS as an voluntary organisation would be very welcome in every district. This can be encouraged looking into their ideology of greater inclination towards producers' welfare through participatory approach. However it can not be made a formal set up. It should be supplementary to the government efforts made towards marketing of IRDP products. Another viable alternative which could be considered is organising DSMS as an integral part of DRDA. However, establishing DSMS as new organisation in addition to the existing agencies providing marketing support and input supply to the IRDP beneficiaries as it may not be economically viable. It is advocated to function as a new supply and marketing cell within DRDA. Since the inflow of funds for proposed DSMS scheme is out of the overall money allocated to IRDP (10% of total), it is felt the DRDAs can have clear accountability to DSMS provided it would be an integral part of it.

There is also a need to lay much emphasis on the 'marketing-mix' of DSMS which constitute production designing, marketing communication (publicity & advertising), branding and packaging, extension education on marketing techniques, pricing method, promotional policies and product placement policies. The DSMS may utilise the existing distribution network in the private sector for more consumer coverage. However, the major task should be conceived to bring the producer and outlets (traders or consumers) closure to each other to realise optimum sales with higher margin of profit. It is anticipated that the DSMS should as a *catalyst* in providing marketing support to the IRDP beneficiaries' products in the overall process. It should not make the beneficiaries dependent on it for a longer period.

By and large, the DSMS may be set up in any firm has to solve the problems prevailing in rural marketing. They are complex and not well-organised to meet its problems. It needs to be re-oriented to overcome the conventional concepts and practices. It has been observed that the changes in social and perceptions often influence the rural markets to a great extent. There are some problems related to the market environment leading to product distribution, promotion and market segmentation. It has been found that the product-market awareness is lacking largely among entrepreneurs and the buyers in rural areas. The communication media is being inadequately used to promote such stimulie. The specific problems encircling the rural markets are as under: (i) Lack of proper procurement planning of raw materials; (ii) Inaccessibility to appropriate markets; (iii) Lack of contemporary product design and packaging techniques; (iv) Poor quality perception for rural products; (v) Lack of quality marketing and testing facilities; (vi) Inadequate facilities in upgrading skills; and (vii) Lack of constant watch on market situations.

Besides, these specific problems the lack of co-ordination among producers, marketing agencies and DRDAs also puse difficulties in setting up marketing network. It is thus essential, to streamline the product-market linkages in IRDP. The IRDP products should fit well with the normal market force and it can not function in isolation. To achieve such market resistance it is required that much emphasis should be given on consumer awareness, qualitative aspects advertisement, branding and packaging. The workshop called upon some management analysis to be done in planning, rural marketing better. The SWOT Strength, Weakness, Opportunity and Threat and PEST Political economic, Social and technological analysis have been recommended for thorough screening of markets before launching the products. However the state intervention through DRDAs need to be thought of carefully with regard to product-market penetrations.

Emerging Issues

The study on different administrative arrangements for setting-up linkages for the beneficiaries assisted under various rural development programmes, projected many issues of economic importance from the overall analysis presented in this report. These issues need substantial discussion and consideration from an applied and perspective angle. The emerging issues are as under:

(i) Whether the existing pattern of linkages in rural industries where the production and marketing activities are at subsistance level, are functioning in the right direction? What motivational, behavioural, administrative coordination and the business logistics approaches need to be considered in rural areas,

(ii) The status of production economy in these firms reveal that they lack in technology adoption, finance and contemporary skills. Under these conditions what should be the role of state intervention in uplifting the rural economy of artisans through organised efforts. There is a need to draw a policy of the government towards upgrading the skills and providing applicable technology at par to their socio-economic conditions,

(iii) The products of beneficiaries assisted under rural development programmes have to build-up resistance to withstand the market competition and sustain therein by adopting appropriate marketing strategies. The link institutions have been providing the management support for production and marketing since 1990. Consequently, such patronage has developed a sense of economic protection among the firm operated by the beneficiaries. In this context, there emerges an issue that how long such protection is required and what are the prerequisites for such firms to establish independently in the open market.

(iv) The promotion of institutional marketing for bulk purchasing of the products from the industrial houses of the beneficiaries need to be developed. The issue of considering the government resolution to make the purchase of rural products mandatory in the government and public sector establishments need to considered as a policy perspective to promote the rural products marketing institutionally. It would be a better option to develop such arrangement as an effective alternative channel and

(v) The cooperative extension work need a dynamic start in rural areas. The NGOs may be entertained in such field where a social and personal approach is required instead of an administrative look out on the development of rural cooperatives.

Policy Perspectives

The market identity crisis starts from production to consumer recognition of the product. The workshop examined the major constraints in product marketing in rural perspective and its impact on the rural economy. There is a need to bridge the gap between the market & the produce to achieve a balance for proper demand & supply. It was noted that to achieve this, the problems need to be identified. However on the existing problems following measures need to be considered[5]:

(i) Organising of one-time shows or melas should be undertaken as it will prove to be more result oriented as the people will be in a buying spree in such festive mood. Besides, the group felt that the routine melas and the marketing outlets of the government do not produce the desired results. Thus the artisan's fairs need to organised with more spatial coverage to strengthen the buyer-seller relationship.

(ii) The state should intervene in marketing of the rural products as there is a problem of time space. It is proposed that state should act as a catalyst in marketing.

(iii) The producers should not entirely depend on the

government support nor totally depend on themselves in the rural marketing at the embryonic stage.

(iv) A single active promoter can boost sales tremendously and so it should be made compulsory to have a single active promotor, for craft or area specific activities.

(v) The trade specific surveys need to be conducted for successful marketing, before hand and the status of venture is to be identified whether it should be a group venture or an individual one.

(vi) Since the heavy competition from large organised sector is also affecting the small rural producers who are not in a position to afford brand & pack their products attractively let aside advertising. Therefore, bottom-up approach and establishment of forward linkages for marketing rural products is suggested, besides participatory approach. In the above context certain other specific problems were identified by the group, as listed below:

(a) lack of facilities for upgrading skills.
(b) absence of proper procurement planning.
(c) absence of onward linkages.
(d) poor quality perception for rural products.
(e) lack of appropriate marketing technology -designing,branding and packaging as a whole.
(f) absence of consumer awareness.
(g) lack of adoptability, accessibility & approachability.
(h) absence of constant watch on market situation.

Backward and Forward Linkages (B & FL)

The arrangements for supply of inputs and marketing support for the products manufactured under RDPs constitute the major backward and forward linkages. The concept of providing institutional linkages emerged in seventh five year plan with the emphasis on DSMS. The strategy perspectives emerged thereby are:·

(i) In context to the long debated issue on planning for B & FL with reference to rural products and urban clientele, the discussion moved around some emerging aspects as what should be structure of an agency providing B & FL. It was agreed that the role of NGOs in building up B & FL would be more result oriented than DSMS under the purview of

DRDA. However it has been suggested that NGO's role should be catalytic in nature rather than sympathetic.

(ii) An active co-ordination between the government departments and bulk consumers for product marketing through the DSMS or NGOs, need to be built up and,

(iii) The NGOs may be involved in conducting consumer survey, to make aware the rural entrepreneurs about the demand. The technical know-how may also be provided with the state-NGO collaboration.

Marketing Policies for Rural Development Programme

Till recently no provision was given for rural marketing and so no proper B & FL have been created in strict sense. In the changing perspectives, the government is giving much attention towards providing marketing support for rural products. In all, three patterns of market segments can be identified in the rural sector.

(1) Marketing of products at local level.
(2) Link up with organisations like commodity corporation etc.
(3) Products having of high demand concentration and excellent quantity.

It is proposed to pay considerable attention on developing rural marketing sector through

(i) existing functional corporations in the region such as KVIC,
(ii) by organising DSMS, and
(iii) mother unit concept in case of certain items such as electronics, carpet weaving etc.

However, the suggestion of the National Productivity council in 1981 to set-up RMSC and DSMS can be accepted institutionally for the following reasons:

(1) to act as a wholesaler
(2) to design brand names etc.
(3) to undertake publicity work.

The DSMS should be provide maximum benefit to the producer and the intervention of government should be limited. Before setting up the DSMS, it is suggested to prepare a project report on Marketing Prospects which can be supplemented by all available schemes to get the optimum results. The traditional activities should be given importance in the process. The DSMS should act as a specialised cell for marketing. However, the financing to the producers can be controlled by DRDAS.

Voluntary agencies with young professionals, should be made to participate in preparing perspective marketing plans. It is felt that there is no specific rural market insulated from the general market. Melas should be organised with the help of voluntary organisations. Nominating one voluntary organisation in each state as a nodal agency for promoting rural marketing would be good proposition. It also suggested that the rural melas should cater to all needy rural producers and should not be limited to IRDP beneficiaries.

Strategy to Evolve Effective Rural Marketing System

It is a challenging task to develop the market for rural products within the territorial and capital limitations. There is a need to insulate the rural products marketing from the open market competition and streamline with changing consumer behaviour. To set market direction for rural products, considerable thinking need to be given towards appropriate planning of marketing strategies. The workshop delineated the following approaches to be considered for building up resistant and efficient marketing system for rural products. The specific suggestions made by the group on this theme are as under:

(1) Building up baseline product marketing infrastructure network with adequate B & FL.

(2) State - patronage need to be essentially planned during the early stages of entrepreneurial firms.

(3) The scope of DSMS need to enhanced. It should cater the needs of all artisans even beyond the IRDP. The DSMS should emerge as a marketing institutions specific to region and potential markets but not to any programme alone.

(4) The DSMS in collaboration with CAPART should organise exhibition and fairs at district level. The NGOs need to be geared up by CAPART for all marketing extension services, and

(5) The DSMS need to shoulder the responsibility of getting popular branding and packaging of rural products and centre into professionalism with least bureaucracy.

The marketing support for the rural artisans identified under the government rural development programmes has been debated since long. However, yet the policy has not been concretised and streamlined for an effective coordination. Of late, the issue of the need for setting-up linkages for the rural productive activities in the non-farm sector has led to a recognition in the political and administrative cliques. The gulf between the business ethics in rural areas and the state intervention need to be bridged to achieve the economic transformation in the rural enterprises.

References

1. Rajagopal : Entrepreneurship and Rural Marketing, Rawat Publications, Jaipur, 1992, pp 30-52.
2. Govt. of India: Draft Seventh Five Year Plan (1985-90), Planning Commission, New Delhi, 1986.
3. National Institute of Rural Development : Status of Institutional Marketing, Background Paper for the Workshop on Business Linked Development Planning, NIRD, September 27-29, 1993.
4. For details see Rajagopal :
   (i) Rural Marketing Management: A case study in Madhya Pradesh, Report, NIRD, 1989
   also see, (ii) Input Supply and Marketing Assistance to IRDP Beneficiaries: A study in Goa State, Report, NIRD, 1992,
   (iii) Rural Marketing Management, Discovery Publishing House, New Delhi, 1994.
5 National Institute of Rural Development : National Seminar on Marketing Support for Rural Development Programmes, September 9-10, 1991. Recommendations, NIRD, Hyderabad, 1991.

2

Rural Marketing Administration

The Concept

The market led economic development is an essential postulate for achieving the employment and income targets in rural areas set in view to alleviate poverty. There are numerous evaluation studies on Integrated Rural Development Programme [IRDP] conducted by government and private researchers being one of the major programmes implemented for rural development. In the past, most of the assessments made by the government have been favourable, but the micro level studies on IRDP have shown alarming results on cost-benefit and income variables. Most of the studies reflected that in absence of an appropriate marketing support system for the products produced by the IRDP beneficiaries, the process of income generation is largely obstructed. The rural industries, dairying, poultry and allied sector have faced the setback in economic growth, due to lack of proper marketing linkages[1]. Thus there emerged the need for a marketing agency to be developed as an institutional outlet for ensuring input supply at reasonable prices and to support marketing of products, produced by the target group. In some states this policy was carried out through NGOs or the existing strength of District Rural Development Agencies (DRDA) as an integral part thereof. They have been functioning as District Supplies and Marketing Societies/Agencies (DSMS)/(DSMA) since the beginning of seventh five year plan as an autonomous agency. These organisations have emerged as a para-development set-up within DRDAs but had always an imperfect organisational anotomy. However, in states like Gujarat and Goa the marketing arrangements for the products of IRDP beneficiaries have been tug-up with voluntary organisation and corporation respectively. In Gujarat, SEWA a voluntary organisation has been linked up for marketing activities where as the Goa Handicrafts, Rural and Small Scale Industries

Development Corporation has been linked with Rural Development Agency for providing marketing support to IRDP beneficiaries.

The Kerala Rural Development and Marketing Society (KERAMS) has been organised in the state in 1986 as an 'apex' society with its branches in districts. Of late, considerable stress has been given by the Union Government in formulating a policy for providing input supply and marketing assistance at state level and has been emphasised in the Seventh Five Year Plan. The major problem in carrying out the implications of the policy has been due to miss-matches production and marketing linkages. It is found that decision for providing marketing support at the time of grounding the unit is not taken which generates marketing gap. Why such decisions are not taken at the time of grounding schemes and what makes it difficult are the debatable issues.

In the rural development programmes the financial assistance and technological extension provided by the government agencies have been production oriented to a large extent. As such, the break-through in development finance has helped in setting-up many new production units like rural industries, dairy units, poultry and fish farms, horticulture farms etc. and also in reviving the traditional occupations prevailing in rural areas. However, it could not help in generating required income for the beneficiaries assisted under different schemes to cross the poverty line. In fact, in absence of proper linkages to market the products produced in the rural areas, the gap in income generation was created[2]. Such problem has largely been observed in IRDP. In fact, it is the basic tool for income generation but in the absence of proper market linkages in IRDP, whether a beneficiary lying below poverty line is 'net benefited'? The question calls for an indepth enquiry into the matter.

The Seventh Five Year Plan envisaged the need for marketing facilities in rural areas. The plan stated that as regards the economic viability of the household enterprises, the major handicaps experienced are pertaining to the supply of raw materials, access to credit and facilities for marketing. As a result there is considerable exploitation of these households by the middlemen. Further, the document adds that the government sponsored programmes for the poor, such as dairy and poultry, account for only a small proportion of total market for such products now, sometimes even less than one per cent.

It has been observed by reviewing the available literature on the linkages in rural development programmes that though the need for providing strong backward and forward linkages for the rural enterprises assisted under various rural development programmes is accepted widely, there is no uniformal pattern emerged so far for the purpose. It has been made a state subject for making suitable administrative and managerial decisions in reference to the local requirement. The policy of DSMS has been formulated by the DRD, Govt. of India for setting-up such societies in all the districts. However, the implementation of the policy has been considered again as state issue. Consequently, there exists different administrative arrangements for providing inputs and marketing assistance to the beneficiaries. The experiments for establishing effective linkages are being carried out with the totally state controlled arrangement, the Khadi and Village Industries Board and the voluntary organisation in Karnataka, Maharashtra and Gujarat respectively. This study analyses the feasibilty and economic viability of such administrative arrangements interms of organisational and functional aspects. It is anticipated that this study will highlight the most appropriate arrangement and draw strategies for 'blue print' approach or identify parametres for the 'green house' approach for extending such arrangements for rural marketing in other states.

It is pointed out in the plan document that the major areas of weakness under IRDP are the absence of infrastructural support, backward and forward linkages. In order to ensure the requirement of programme specific and general infrastructure at local level, funds were provided separately, over and above the subsidy funds, as a part of the overall outlay under IRDP. These funds, among other things were earmarked for utilisation in developing institutions such as 'District Supplies and Marketing Societies' (DSMS) at district level to take care of raw materials, input requirements and out put marketing. It is further envisaged that an infrastructure sub-plan should be prepared as an integral part of the sub-sectoral district plans[3].

During the Seventh Five Year Plan period, the concept of DSMS was not taken-up with zest by all the state governments.

Consequently, such an institution for marketing support emerged only in few states. Of these, Kerala made a headway by organising such society at 'Apex' level as Kerala Rural Development and Marketing Society (KERAMS) with its branches at district level. It may also be noted that a similar kind of approach was followed in Sixth plan period as 'Single Window System' at district level but it had a major criticism, of absence of marketing facilities for majority of commodities produced in various sectors.

Revised DSMS Policy

The experience of implementation of IRDP as one of the major programmes on poverty alleviation revealed that over the decade there has been shift in the activities financed under the programme away from the primary sector to the secondary and tertiary sector. This change in the development trend has accentuated the need for ensuring proper marketing arrangements for the goods and services transacted in the rural - urban areas. The introduction of Development of Women and Children in Rural Areas (DWCRA) in 1982 has further stressed the need to for institutional marketing in view to support the input supply and output marketing of various economic activities taken-up under DWCRA scheme[4]. As stated in the pre text various evaluation studies have also pointed the marketing gap as one of the major factors in not achieving the established objectives of various development programmes including IRDP to a large extent. The failure of DSMS scheme formulated in early eighties had also been the reason for marking slow growth in rural development till the end of Seventh Five Year Plan. Consequently the Government of India has revised the DSMS policy with view to enhance the scope of its operation and budgetory provisions[5].

The document emphasises that the DSMS should provide integrated service to the IRDP beneficiaries in the cottage and rural industries sector in respect of supply of raw materials, marketing of surplus products, information on technological upgradation and extension of credit support. The specific functions of the DSMS has been identified as under[6]:

1. To conduct surveys associated District Industries Centres in order to obtain information regarding the status of supply

of raw materials for rural industries and their product marketing.

2. To set-up suitable display and sales centres in an urban area and develop it as multy-commodity emporium.
3. To ensure marketing of maximum 50 per cent of the products manufactured by the beneficiaries and leaving the other half to be marketed by themselves in the open market.
4. To set-up godowns for storage of finished products and raw materials.
5. To identify the markets outside the hinterland.
6. To assess consumer demand for the products, ensure quality control and supply on time.
7. To lay down standards specifications for the goods produces in the cottage and rural industries sector.
8. To provide institutional support to the units for getting credit support for upgradation of units through the state and central governments, and public sector undertakings.
9. To maintain institutional linkages with potential marketing organisations.
10. To utilise the channel of Public Distribution System and also Private Channels for marketing of rural products.
11. To provide support in collaboration with the Rural Training Centres for skill development, technology transfer and quality testing of products.
12. To obtain soft loan from the financial institutions on the pattern of Handloom Cooperatives on concessional rates of interest under section 17 of RBI Act.
13. To coordinate with the existing institutional marketing organisations for improving the sales status of rural products.
14. To set-up sub-centres in the areas of marketing gap.
15. To use the research and financial institutions for conducting consumer and market surveys.
16. To enable DRDAs to establish counters for marketing of IRDP/DWCRA products in the districts and other areas of economic concern.
17. The DSMS should draw margin money for obtaining soft loans from the financial institutions.
18. To establish links with the defence, para-military, police, schools, hostels etc. for supplying the consumer durables

manufactured by the beneficiaries. The product may range handlooms, carpentary items, pottery, bamboo products, garments, carpets and the like.

19. To develop cooperative super stores.
20. To draw marketing assistance from the Council of Advancement of Peoples Action and Rural Technology (CAPART) in organising superstores in large towns.
21. Networking with the district administration in developing marketing links with the other institutions.
22. The DSMS should also support funds for development of village markets held periodically.

It is suggested that the DSMS should generally be a cooperative body registered under the societies act. However, in exceptional cases where there is not a healthy environment for organising the cooperatives it may be registered as a corporation or a voluntary agency[7]. The decision in this regard should be taken in consultation with the state government. The budgetary provisions for the DSMS is enhanced to Rs. 1 Million (Rs. 10 lakhs) from the earlier provision of 0. 3 Millions. The detailed financial outlay will be as under:

Amount in Lakhs

1.	Rent for premises for 3 years (a) sales emporium) (b) Godown)	Rs	1. 80
2.	Pre-requirement of samples	Rs	0. 40
3.	Seed Capital	Rs	5. 00
4.	Fixtures and Furnishings	Rs	0. 80
5.	Managerial Subsidy	Rs	2. 00
	Total Budget Provisioned	Rs	10. 00

The seed capital would constitute the initial funding to DSMS. It could be stepped-up from time to time so as to represent 50 per cent of the total working capital requirements of the society. However, it could increase with the rise in turnover of the organisation.

Institutional Networking in Marketing

In recent development an integrated system of backward and forward linkages have been established in Karnataka to support the economic reformation of rural artisans in true sense. The VISWA programme designed and implemented by the Karnataka government sets a clear distinction between the myth and reality of rural economic development by generating additional employment and income at the grass roots. The system involves the sectoral corporations and boards for providing inputs, technology, trainning, finance and marketing support to the beneficiaries. It is in this background the government of Karnataka has attempted to implement a continuous rural productive employment programme in the fall of 1990, named as VISHWA.

The states enjoyed the discretion on making arrangements for maketing of the products manufactured by the beneficiaries assisted under IRDP and DWCRA programmes in their state, subject to the convenience of their administrative set-up and the anticipated expenditure in handling such additional workload. Thus, we do not find any uniformity in the marketing arrangement made for the products as RDPs in rural areas across the states. Consequently, in Maharashtra the State Khadi and Village Industries Board is providing the inputs and marketing assistance to the beneficiaries of RDPs engaged in the rural industries sector. The KVIB functions with the revolving fund made available through the state government for establishing backward and forward linkages. However, in Gujarat the Self Employed Womens' Association [SEWA], a voluntary organisation is offering only the marketing assistance in Banaskantha district through their outlets in many parts of the state. The government has made this arrangement to study the system on pilot basis.

The DSMS co-exists in Karnataka state but its role seems to be not effective as compared to the sectoral corporations which could establish input supply and marketing linkages under the VISWA programme[8]. However, the DSMS caters to the marketing needs of limited commodities. Due to various organisational constraints it is unable to expand the marketing activities for majority of the commodities produced by the target group beneficiaries assisted under various programmes in the district. The major problems experienced by the officers in making their unit viable are in relation to the availability of supporting services and infrastructural facilities like, marketing, input availability, repair and maintenance facilities, worksheds etc[9]. The foregoing text details the administrative arrangements made for the marketing of rural products manufactured by the beneficiaries of different rural development programmes in the states of Karnataka, Maharashtra and Gujarat[10].

Methodology

Study Area

The study was undertaken in the three states namely Karnataka, Maharashtra and Gujarat where three different types of administrative arrangements are existing. Table 2.1 shows the type of institutions involved in providing linkages and their status in the selected states.

Table 2.1: Administrative Network for Linkages in Study Area

Sl No.	*State*	*Institutional Tie-up*	*Status*
1.	Karnataka	Sectoral Corporations and Boards linked with VISWA Programme of State Govt.	State programme but link instts are autonomous
2.	Maharashtra	Maharashtra State Khadi & Village Industries Board	Autonomous
3.	Gujarat	Self Employed Womens' Association	Voluntary Organisation

One district in each state has been selected where the procurement and sales were highest. In case of Banaskantha district of Gujarat, there was no choice as the government attempted the linkage with SEWA for providing inputs and marketing support to the IRDP beneficiaries on a pilot basis. In the states of Karnataka and Maharashtra the Mysore and Kolhapur districts were selected. The primary data has been collected from 100 beneficiaries in each district by administering a pre-coded structured schedule. As large as 300 beneficiaries have been canvassed for collection the primary data. However, due to paucity of information 10 observations are deleted from the analysis. In all the three states in the selected districts, 290 beneficiaries have been covered in the study spread over 25 villages in the 07 talukas engaged in the 13 different economic activities.

Organisational Approaches

In Andhra Pradesh, Karnataka, Tamilnadu, Kerala, Gujarat and Goa such experiments have been carried out in some districts establishing an institutional linkage to serve as a facilitator for enrouting the products in the open market and regulating the credit provided to the beneficiaries. These institutions are organised on the lines of DSMS and function as an integrated part of District Rural Development Agencies, corporations and voluntary organisations. They are autonomous bodies catering the input supply and marketing assistance to the beneficiaries assisted under IRDP and DWCRA programmes. Table 2.2 exhibits the pattern of institutional linkages established with reference to different programmes being implemented therein.

Table 2. 2: Institutional Linkages Across States

Sl No.	State	Programme	Institutional Linkages	
			Activity	Institution
1.	Karnataka	VISHWA, IRDP	Leather Goods	LIDKAR
			Carpentry	DSMS
			Mat Weaving	DSMS
			Rosewood Inlay & Carving	KSHDC
			Handloom	KHDC
			Gem Cutting	DGDC
2.	Maharashtra	IRDP	Leather Goods	KVIB
			Garments	Coops
3.	Gujarat	DWCRA	Embroidery	SEWA
			Leather Work	SEWA
			Patch Work	SEWA
			Weaving	SEWA

It is observed in Karnataka the backward and forward linkages have been established in a multi-agency administrative frame involving the sectoral corporations and boards and is being integrated and monitored by the District Industries Centres at district level. The system involves the sectoral corporations and boards for providing inputs, training, finance and marketing support to the beneficiaries. It is in this background, the government of Karna.aka has attempted to implement a continuous rural productive employment programme in the fall of 1990. The credit assistance has been provided by the Karnataka State Financial Corporation linking the trainning, production and marketing responsibilities with the sectoral departments like development of leather artisans with LIDKAR, gem cutting artisans with DGDC, rural mat weavers and carpenters with DSMS, handloom and silk weavers with KHDC and artisans producing handicrafts with the Karnataka State Handicrafts Development Corporation. The inputs are supplied by these agencies and also the output is marketed through their emporia. The loan is recovered by these agencies while making payment for the procured products to the artisans. It is termed as *'loan deduction at source'*. In this manner the credit-marketing coordination is established in the VISHWA programme of the state.

On the contrary in Maharashtra there exists the double-agency system consisting of DRDA and KVIB. The former agency provides trainning, infrastructure, subsidy and logistic support while the latter renders the assistance for input supply and output marketing. However, the DRDA coordinates with the financing agencies to arrange for credit to the beneficiaries. The mono-agency system of integrated linkages exists in the Banaskantha district of Gujarat where SEWA provides the organisational and functional support to the rural women engaged in various economic activities. The SEWA organises the rural women into informal groups, provides trainning through the government assisted programmes, renders the technological support and provides an assured market for the goods manufactured by the groups. However, the revolving fund of Rs 15, 000. 00 is paid through SEWA to the informal groups for use as working capital.

VISHWA Approach in Karnataka

As stated in the pre-text there is a multi-agency approach followed in Karnataka state to provide the backward and forward linkages to the beneficiaries identified under the

VISHWA schemes on the lines of IRDP criteria. The specific parametres for selection of beneficiaries under this programme include (i) persons in the age group of 18-35 with or without formal education (ii) persons who are unemployed or under employed and (iii) rural youths already trained under the government sponsored programmes in addition to the IRDP guidelines set for the identification.

Government of Karnataka after examining the need to provide an integrated support mechanism for generating continuous rural productive employment through efficient institutional linkages has constituted four committees to evolve strong organisational structure for policy making and implementation of the VISHWA programme. The organisational system is largely top-down system in which the policy is decided at the high level committees and the directives pass through the intermediate levels which endorse the feasibility of centralised guidance. The district tier is conceived as the policy implementing unit in the whole organisational system and is the agency to draw sectoral coordination on backward and forward linkages from the sectoral department at the grass roots level.

The high level committee comprises the Cabinet Ministers in charge of major ministries like education, revenue, planning and institutional finance, housing and urban development, industries, social welfare, science and technology, ecology and environment and sericulture. The Ministers of State comprising the small scale industries, labour, forest, veterinary, fisheries and ports and horticulture ministries. Besides, the key administrators are also included in the committee of First Order. The guidelines formulation, budgetary consideration for the programme and reviewing the progress made at the district levels are the major functions under the purview of the high level committee.

The Committees at the level II and III concentrates largely on the administrative matters for effective implementation of the programme. The district level committee in the selected Mysore district shoulders the whole responsibility of establishing credit, technology and marketing linkages with the rural enterprises by coordinating with the sectoral departments. At the district level the Chief Secretary of Zilla Parishad is the controlling authority of the VISHWA programme while the General Manager, District Industries Centre acts as executive authority for establishing the linkages and coordination. However, it is observed that there is no peoples' participation at the lower level committees though the programme claims to be rural artisans oriented and need based. The participation of beneficiaries or village leaders would have been helpful in appropriate planning for products, technology and marketing aspects considering the entrepreneurial perceptions.

Institutional Linkage in Maharashtra

There is bi-institutional linkage system exists in the Kolhapur district of Maharashtra. The DRDA does the prescribed procedure for providing financial assistance to the beneficiaries under IRDP right from identification to the releases of subsidy. The beneficiaries are also provided training prior to start of the unit. The KVIB is linked to the beneficiaries for the purpose of input supply and marketing assistance. Such administrative arrangement has been made by the Government of Maharashtra throughout the state by releasing substantial revolving fund to the KVIB for supplying them the required raw material on payment and procurring the finished products from the beneficiaries. The KVIB has a network of emporia throughout the state to market the procured product. However, the surplus production on the beneficiaries own raw material is largely sold in the weekly markets held in the villages by the beneficiaries themselves.

Such arrangement in the district has been made since 1990. There are many activities covered under this linkage like handlooms, polyester khadi, basketry, agarbatti making, handicrafts, honey, processed food products and the like but in the district the KVIB is concentrating only on the leather goods as it is a traditionally grown activity which has been recognised in the country under the brand name of 'Kolhapuri Chappals and Bags'. The KVIB finds no market risk in dealing with this product as it has acquired widely the consumer recognition. The KVIB also sells the products through the emporia certified by the Khadi and Village Commission [KVIC] on consignment basis throughout the country. Thus the KVIC has shown good progress in procurement and sales of leather goods manufactured by the IRDP beneficiaries. Thus the KVIC also form an indirect linkage in the forward trade of the products procured by the KVIB.

SEWA in Gujarat

SEWA — a voluntary organisation, has been organising the rural poor, beneficiaries of the government sponsored programmes and the self employed women engages in various economic activities in rural and urban areas in Gujarat. This association has been instrumental to promote the cooperative spirit among the women entrepreneurs working in a large unorganised sector and makes them aware of their worker-producer role in bridging the gulf of economic inequality in the business oriented activities. Since September 1988, SEWA is working on a regional development programme conceived indigenously, in the Sultanpur and Radhapur talukas of the Banaskantha district of Gujarat. The State Government in the year 1990 negotiated with the association to provide the marketing support to the women beneficiaries assisted under DWCRA programme on pilot basis in the Banaskantha district.

The acceptance of the responsibility of rendering the marketing support the endeavour to establish linkages for input supply and marketing assistance to the beneficiaries of DWCRA began in the state. Since the SEWA has experienced years with the rural women and synthesised the psycho-social aspect of their living, it takes-up the lead to form the informal and formal groups of economic activities, provides linkages and monitors their progress. However, the government, provides the financial support to the DWCRA groups and coordinates with the systems approach of SEWA. In planning through the Bottom-up Approach there are four principal components need to be considered. They are, The Economic Urge, The Process, The Strategy and The Environment emerging responsible for the formation of an economic group. The economic urge is the component that considers the peoples' need, values, anticipations and the ability to contribute in terms of production to meet the needs. The process is largely associated with the behavioural dimensions of the urge and the strategy is an outcome of the positive interaction of the first two components. The environment, of course is a governing component which deals with the external factors like state intervention, market competition and technology development.

It is observed during the study that all the activities promoted by SEWA through the DWCRA groups have attained substantial resistance to withstand the open market environmental changes, risks and uncertainities. The approaches followed by SEWA in indentifying the economic activity, formation of groups, intra-group portfolio management, training needs etc are largely participatory. It can be stated that system followed by the association is Bottom-up Approach and involves the people mentally and physically in streamlining the economic enterprise for a common interest.

The SEWA coordinates with the taluka, block and panchayat administrations for conducting the base line survey of the rural women lying below poverty line and the traditional economic activities in vogue. The block level committees of SEWA prepares the list of identified beneficiaries specifying their economic activity of the craft.

The overall list of working women is prepared and submitted by the SEWA workers to the Block Development Office and from this IRDP beneficiary list, a craftwise member list is drawn out. SEWA makes thorough attempt on discussing the scheme taken up for the rural women at the village level and seeks individual endorsement on the same in respect of concept, approach, members involvement and the extent of benefits. Such process paves the distance between the formal administrative approach and the grass-roots anticipations. The womens groups are formed for specific activities on arriving at concensus in the Gram Sabha meetings. The skill development is one of the important factors considered by the SEWA as it has direct bearing on the per capita productivity of the members. The decisions on the productivity linked tarinning needs are discussed at the block and district levels with the representation of women entrepreneurs in all the meetings. The group leaders are also given induction trainning on leadership development for making them firm on managing the groups successfully. It is observed that one of the significant outcomes of the informal groups organised for income and employment generating activities is towards their Human Output which helps in increasing the business efficiency in many ways.

In the group approach, the growth of human outputs is reflected in terms of clarity of goals, approach, motivation, commitment, behavioural adjustments, clarity in business logistics and awareness of personal and organisational realities.

The human output also contributes to many behaviours and interactions that are required to manage and run the group. It is not possible to give an exhaustive list of variables that are simultaneously developed in the process of group dynamics. They are the qualities of leadership and supervision leading to market leader in the long run, inter-group relation and professional integration, participation in the problem clinics and conflict management issues at par with other group members, decision making and planning. Besides the group approach in rural business provides self confidence among the entrepreneurs as the group action is periodically appraised in which every member participates. Such group dynamics in rural marketing develops interpersonal relationship and a social control over the entire process. However, the economic gains account to the net profit, returns on investment, rate of growth of production, employment and the cost effectiveness. The economic gains have also some social implications such as increase in the quality of work and life index, awareness, sustainability of the rural marketing in competitive environment and rise in the bargaining power.

In context to the rural business the group dynamics has considerable role to play in maximising the profit by shortening the intermediate links. It is regarded as an effective instrument for developing strong bargaining power in the competitive market environment, mobilise consensus to resist external forces acting against the economic interest of the people. In all it can be stated that the process of group dynamism develops business logistics in marketing of indegenous products of the hinterland and affirms the resistence to the risk and uncertainty anticipated by an individual entrepreneur.

In the overall excercise of Bottom-up Approach the opinion of members of Gram Sabha is considered as instrumental in formation of the groups, providing productive and managerial trainning to the members and group leaders. It can be stated that the organisational structure of backward and forward linkages for the rural enterprises assisted under IRDP and DWCRA in Gujarat represent the peoples participation in strict socio-economic sense.

Functional Efficiency

The production and investment pattern in ISB sector determines the product type and quantity to be manufactured, its design and quality. However the excercise on environmental mapping will help to identify the markets for the product of rural origin - hinterland, intra- and inter state markets and export. It can be stated that the production system should necessarily have the association with the market environment for a sustained life cycle of a firm generating conteneous production, income and employment in the REFs. The production of need based commodities in rural areas always create large markets. It is observed during the study that the handlooms and bamboo products in Mysore. Leather goods in Mysore and Kolhapur districts and embroidery, patch work etc. in the Banaskantha district cater the consumer and industrial needs to a large extent. However, the commodities produced in other trades have substantial market for the consumers of high income bracket. Such goods include sandalwood, rosewood and inlay work pieces manufactured by the VISHWA beneficiaries in the Mysore district.

Investment Pattern

It was observed during the study that a major portion of financial requirement for. establishing the unit is met by the commercial banks and DRDAs under IRDP and DWCRA programmes in Maharashtra and Gujarat states. However, in case of investment gap a meagre amount is invested out of own capital or borrowed from the informal sources by the leather artisans in Kolhapur district and women's group in Banaskantha district. In fact the amount of loan provided under IRDP or DWCRA in the form of revolving fund for grounding of different schemes is utilised by the beneficiaries towards meeting the requirements such as raw materials, infrastructure etc. in the initial stages for setting up the unit. In case of group assistance under DWCRA, each entrepreneure has been provided Rs. 1000 on an average for a group of 15 members. It was stated by 26.27 per cent of the beneficiaries engaged in embroidery, mirror and patchwork in the Banaskantha district that they require amount frequently for procurement of raw materials. However SEWA has shown positive sign to provide additional amount for working capital from the Womens Cooperative Bank, if a joint committee of group leader and SEWA organisers feel so. The amount disbursed is lower than the amount of loan applied for by the beneficiaries. The data reveals that there is also a difference in the amount of loan sanctioned and disbursed. On an average 17.91 per cent less amount was sanctioned to the beneficiaries over the amount applied for. The loan amount was disbursed in two or three phases to the beneficiaries according to the growing financial requirements of unit in all the three selected districts. The disbursement of loan has been controlled by the Joint Monitoring Committee constituting different officials in each of the selected districts as given below :

[1] Mysore District: District Industries Centre, Sectoral Corporations and Karnataka State Financial Corporation

[2] Kolhapur District: Industrial Extn. Officers (KVIB) and DRDA Officials

[3] Banaskantha District: Group Leader, SEWA Organiser and Block Development Officer or Mukhya Sevika [Women & Child]

The full amount of loan was not disbursed at once for the two reasons, (i) either the loan amount disbursed to the unit was sufficient to ground and operate the scheme or (ii) it has been withheld to streamline the production, marketing and repayment factors of an enterprise. It was observed that under such circumstances the beneficiary who required supply of raw material in regular intervals for the production in the units of basketry fibre, readymade garments and processed food units which had not reached to the break even point (BEP) were bound to arrange for additional investment from other sources. Such instances were observed in the case of wood building material manufacturing beneficiaries under the VISHWA programme who were linked with the DSMS in the Vyasarajapura village in the T Narsipatana Taluka. The 10 beneficiaries engagesd in this economic activity had put 10 per cent of additional working capital over the total disbursed amount of Rs 3000 per beneficiary from the informal money market.

It can be seen from the data that only 10 per cent of additional investment could be made by the entrepreneurs on an average over and above the assistance received from the government sources. The own investments are made out of limited savings and informally borrowed capital. The Table 2.3 exhibits the borrowing pattern of beneficiaries from the private sources. The data reveals that the beneficiaries engaged in manufacturing the wooden building materials in Mysore and leather goods in Kolhapur districts required additional capital to run the unit and borrowed loan from different sources. The beneficiaries engaged in manufacturing leather goods required higher additional loan amount as compared to other entrepreneurs as their productivity is found higher and have been widely recognised in the whole country markets and also possess the export potential. The middlemen and wholesale agents dealing in such products often provide credit interms of raw material etc. to the entrepreneurs the value of which has to be repaid in weekly instalments or adjusted in supplies of finished products.

Table 2.3: Non-Institutional Investment Sources

Sl No	*District*	*Trade*	*No. of Benefi-ciaries*	*Average Amount [Rs.]*	*Source*
1.	Mysore	Carpentry	10	300. 00	Large Farmers
2.	Kolhapur	Leather Goods	18	540. 00	Middlemen and Wholesale agents in the district

The supply of inputs is an important linkage in the overall economy of a rural entrepreneurial firm. The consumer behaviour and market potential largely depend on the quality and quantity of the production. These two factors have various other determinents like infrastructure, technology, knowledge attitude and practising ability (KAP) etc. The production infrastructure consists of availability of raw material, plant and machinery, energy and the available technology. In all, it was found capital intensive machineries are made available to the beneficiaries of gem cutting, leather industry and inlay workers by the link institutions under VISHWA programme in Mysore district. However, the rural entrepreneurial firms in Kolhapur district had all required infrastructure for production. The raw material was locally available. However it was supplied by the link institutions in all the districts under study at the work places of the beneficiaries. It was found during the study that as many as 95.37 per cent entrepreneurs get the raw material through link institutions. There is a quest for raw material in the open market when there is short supply of indented quality and quantity by the link institutions.

Table 2.4 depicts status of net income generation among entrepreneurs engaged in different trades. The data reveals that 36.55 per cent beneficiaries earn between the income range of up to Rs. 500 per month. However, only 16.90 per cent beneficiaries have higher income ranging Rs.1000-2000 per month. Besides, 46.55 per cent of beneficiaries generate income up to Rs. 501-1000 per month only.

Table 2.4: Activity-wise Income Earned by the Beneficiaries in the Selected Disrticts [Rs. per Month]

Sl No	*State District*	*Activity*	*Income Range*			*No of Beneficiaries*
			Up to 500	*501-1000*	*1001-2000*	
1.	Karnataka [Mysore]	Carpentry	08 [80.0]	02 [20.0]	—	10
		Handloom	—	12 [66.7]	06 [33.3]	18
		Leather	06 [24.0]	16 [64.0]	03 [12. 0]	25
		Mat Weaving	02 [18.2]	09 [81.8]	—	11
		Inlay Workers	—	14 [56.0]	11 [44.0]	25
		Gem Cutting	—	18 [72.0]	07 [28.0]	25
2.	Maharashtra [Kolhapur]	Leather	—	34 [60.7]	22 [39.3]	56
		Bamboo Workers	15 [100]	—	—	15
		Handlooms	07 [46.7]	08 [53.3]	—	15
3.	Gujarat [Banaskantha]	DWCRA Groups	68 [75.6]	22 [24.4]	—	90

It can be seen from the above Table the DWCRA groups engaged in embroidery, mirror work and patch work in the Banaskantha district are the lowest income generating groups as compared to the beneficiaries of Mysore and Kolhapur districts under study. One of the reasons largely associated with this characteristic is the limited efforts to tap the market potential for the products within and out side the state.

Trade Practice

As discussed in the pre-text, there are many channels involved in procurement and marketing of products of REFs in the study region. It is observed during the study that the beneficiaries select the channel for marketing based on the mobility and user orientation of the product. For instance, the bamboo and cane products of course quality viz. storage bins, mats etc. are sold either directly to the consumer or to the itinerant traders who in turn sell them in different village markets but the leather products are sold to contractors or wholesalers because of high mobility of the product in the town markets as channelised by them. Table 2.5 exhibits the marketing practices adopted in sale of different kinds of products.

Table 2.5: Product Movement Through Different Channels in Kolhapur District
[Product Value in Per cent to Total Sales per Month]

S.No	*Trade/ Channel*	*Direct*	*Institutional*	*Contractors*
1.	Leather Goods	42.93	57.07	—
2.	Bamboo Products	74.81	—	25.19
3.	Handlooms	64.44	21.69	09.87
	Overall	62.06	39.38	17.53

The data reveals that the beneficiaries largely prefer to sell the products directly to the consumers. However, the institutional channel provides scope for marketing of leather goods and Khadi clothes produced by the beneficiaries. However, the wholesalers who act as contractor procure the products to the extent of 17.53 per cent to the total value of maketable surplus from the beneficiaries.

It has been observed during the study that the beneficiaries assisted under VISHWA programme in Karnataka have quick turnover of stock as the time taken for lifting the products from the workplaces by the institutional agencies is prompt whereas the beneficiaries themselves have to deliver the goods to the

SEWA outlets and KVIB district emporia in Kolhapur. However, there always exists an immediate local market for such products and the entrepreneurs need not necessarily wait for the consignment orders from SEWA. The products of the VISHWA beneficiaries are lifted within 45 of production days on an average. Table 2.6 depicts the time taken for production and supplies to different channels by the beneficiaries engaged in various trades.

Table 2.6: Turnover of Products under Institutional Linkages

[Time in days]

Sl No	*Institutional Linkages*	*Time taken to lift the products*	*Time taken for making payments*
1.	VISHWA	45	07
2.	DRDA - KVIB	30	10
3.	SEWA	07	00

The time taken for despatching the onward consignment by the link institutions require grading, packaging and transportation of the products. The SEWA organisers pay the amount immediately while the KVIB takes longer time to make the payments to the artisans due to procedural delays. In case of the VISHWA beneficiaries the transport is provided by the concerned corporation.

It has been highlighted in some of the similar studies conducted in different parts of the country that there would be higher inclination of entrepreneurs towards institutional channels due to assured marketing support and economic patronage. Thus, the Table 2.7 endorses that large number of entrepreneurs prefer to deliver the product to the link institutions. There are many reasons for selling the products through institutional channels.

The data reveals that the major consideration for mobilising the products through institutional channels is their promptness in the procurement of products form the work places of the beneficiaries. It has been endorsed by 83.10 per cent beneficiaries under study in all the three district. The price spread or the cost of marketing has an important consideration in pricing and profit mechanisms.

Table 2.7: Preference Parametres for the Link Institutions

Sl	*Parametre/District*	*Mysore*	*Kolhapur*	*Banaskantha*	*Total*
1.	Satisfactory Price	98 [85.96]	39 [45.35]	74 [82.22]	211 [72.76]
2.	Graded Price	104 [91.23]	40 [46.51]	82 [91.11]	226 [77.93]
3.	Timely Payment	87 [76.31]	28 [32.56]	90 [100]	205 [70. 69]
4.	Bulk Procurement	63 [55.26]	35 [40.69]	38 [42.22]	136 [46.89]
5.	Quick Lifting	109 [95.61]	46 [53.49]	86 [95.55]	241 [83.10]
	Total Respondents	114	86	90	290

Table 2.8: Price Spread* in Different Institutional Linkages

Sl No	*Institutional Linkages*	*Total Cost of Marketing [Rs/Month]*	*Price Spread [%]*		
			Trans-port	*Storage*	*Middlemen Margin*
1.	VISHWA	—	—	—	—
2.	DRDA - KVIB	142.81	39.61	4.02	36.97
3.	SEWA	122.64	33.54	4.93	—

* Average to the total sample size in respect of the linkages followed in the districts under study.

The price spread includes the cost incurred towards transportation, storage, middlemen's margin, communication etc. in mobilising the product for sale in the market through the opted channel of marketing. The Table 2.8 exhibits the price spread in different constituents and their respective shares.

The share of transportation in price spread consists of 36.57 per cent on an average. It is found during the study that the VISHWA beneficiaries do not spend any amount on marketing for the reasons: (i) the product is lifted immediately by the concerned corporations (ii) The products are stored in the godowns of the institutions providing marketing support and (iii) there are no middlemen involved.

As stated in the pre-text, some of the beneficiaries engaged in leather products, bamboo products and handloom weaving in the Kolhapur district sell their products through the contractors or middlemen with view to accelerate the turnover and meet the immediate need of money. Since the level of production is relatively low in Kolhapur district they require quick recycling of money for consumption and further investment. Under such circumstances, the entrepreneurs try to sell the products immediately without storing them for a better market gain. The private traders initially offer low prices for the products of beneficiaries. However, the price is finally settled through bargaining and negotiations.

Institutional Efficiency

The policy of institutional arrangements for the rural products marketing manufactured by the beneficiaries of various rural development programmes has been a milestone in integrated development efforts put in the rural industries sector. It has emerged from the synchronised pre- and post production factors required for a normal firm under competitive economic conditions. It has been found that there are many factors which have been contributed to the firms' economic and marketing conditions. However, the institutional approach to provide backward and forward linkage to the rural firms has been found an encouragement in all the three kinds of linkages studied with reference to VISHWA, DRDA-KVIB and SEWA. The Table 2.9 exhibits the ranking of these institutional arangements considering the vital economic, marketing and behavioural parametres.

The institutional efficiency is ranked using the formula of composit indexing as under:

$$R = R_i/N_l$$

where,

R = Final Rank

R_i = Sum of rank values and

N_i = Total number of indicators

It can be seen from the Table 2.9 that the VISHWA programme and the linkage with SEWA have been rated as first and the DRDA-KVIB linkage as second. It indicates that the

VISHWA and the SEWA tie-ups have been well conceived by the beneficiaries and are leading to success.

Table 2.9: Efficiency of Institutional Linkages

[Assessment in per cent]

Sl No	Parametres	VISHWA	DRDA-KVIB	SEWA
1.	Product Identification	89.47 [1]	41.86 [3]	80.0 [2]
2.	Skill Development	85.96 [2]	25.58 [3]	86.67 [1]
3.	Procurement	95.61 [1]	53.49 [3]	95. 56 [2]
4.	Pricing	88.59 [1]	46.51 [3]	86.67 [2]
5.	Payment of Wages/ Product Prices	76.31 [2]	32.56 [3]	100.0 [1]
6.	Credit-Marketing Linkage	100.0 [1]	—	24.44 [2]
7.	Environmental Mapping	78.07 [2]	13.95 [3]	84.44 [1]
8.	Awareness Building	86.84 [2]	62.95 [3]	87.78 [1]
9.	Infrastructure	92.98 [1]	75.55 [2]	75.55 [2]
10.	Work Participation	96.49 [2]	56.97 [3]	100.0 [1]
	Composit Index	1.5	2.6	1.5
	Final Ranks	1	2	1

Emerging Issues

The study on different administrative arrangements for setting-up linkages for the beneficiaries assisted under various rural development programmes, projected many issues of economic importance from the overall analysis presented in this report. These issues need substantial discussion and consideration from an applied and perspective angle. The emerging issues are as under:

(i) Whether the existing pattern of linkages in rural industries where the production and marketing activities are at subsistance level, are functioning in the right direction? What motivational, behavioural, administrative coordination and the business logistics approaches need to be considered in rural areas,

(ii) The status of production economy in these firms reveal that they lack in technology adoption, finance and contemporary skills. Under these conditions what should be the role of state intervention in uplifting the rural economy of artisans through organised efforts. There is a need to draw a policy of the government towards upgrading the skills and providing applicable technology at par to their socio economic conditions,

(iii) The products of beneficiaries assisted under rural development programmes have to build-up resistance to withstand the market competition and sustain therein by adopting appropriate marketing strategies. The link institutions have been providing the management support for production and marketing since 1990. Consequently, such patronage has developed a sense of economic protection among the firm operated by the beneficiaries. In this context, there emerges an issue that how long such protection is required and what are the prerequisites for such firms to establish independently in the open market.

(iv) The promotion of institutional marketing for bulk purchasing of the products from the industrial houses of the beneficiaries need to be developed. The issue of considering the government resolution to make the purchase of rural products mandatory in the government and public sector establishments need to considered as a policy perspective to promote the rural products marketing institutionally. It would be a better option to develop such arrangement as an effective alternative channel and

(v) The cooperative extension work need a dynamic start in rural areas. The NGOs may be entertained in such field where a social and personal approach is required instead of an administrative look out on the development of rural cooperatives.

Future Threats

Conceptually marketing is a function of demand and supply, for the products produced in a given space and time. It has different area specific, product specific and socio-cultural characteristics, which determine the product's standing in the market. These factors, by and large govern the trade practice in the markets held in a particular region. However, this may change time and again according to the buyer's and seller's perception towards the marketing efficiency. The rural entrepreneurs, who are the basic suppliers of raw materials to some of the farm and non-farm industries, largely transact in rural markets with small quantities of marketable surplus. They could earn a small margin of profit which covers their subsistance needs. Such economic conditions, limit the extent of capital investment though it may be potentially profitable to invest more. However, at the same time the business ventures are more risky. This is one of the consequences of the area specific characteristic of the market. Likewise, product specific market conditions reflect highly favourable opportunities for maximum sales realisation when the buyers are elite and the sellers have more prolific ways of communicating the product. Besides, the branding and packaging of the product is also important in marketing and this can be popularised through the communication approaches. In modern marketing system, the Approachability, Accessibility, and Adaptability constitute the core strategy for product marketing. The 3A's determine efficiency of product marketing, irrespective of area specifications — rural or urban. The urban markets, largely in private and corporate sectors have been fast developing ever since the marketing communication devises emerged in the trade-world. Apart from strong communication approaches, the product markets are capital oriented and can withstand short run and casual market risks. The use of selling method by price mechanism has been another important aspect of penetrating the products into the competitive markets. The urban markets, with such, manifold characteristics, which are organised to a large extent impose social and economic threats to the rural unorganised markets. Of these, the major threat is of the product saleability in urban market environment. The threats to the rural product markets are also pertaining to their viability and sustainability.

References

1. Subbarao K & Kakawani N : Rural Poverty and Its Alleviation in India, Economic and Political Weekly, March 31, 1991, pp 4-12.

2. Rajagopal : Rural Marketing : Gulf Between the Policy and Practice, Financial Express, p. 9, Jan 06, 1992.
3. Govt. of India : Sixth Five Year Plan, 1985-90, Planning Commission, New Delhi, 1986.
4. Rajagopal : Entrepreneurship and Rural Markets, Rawat Publications, Jaipur, 1992, pp 14-18.
5. Rajagopal : Organising Rural Business : Policy, Planning and Management, SAGE Publications, 1993 (under print).
6. Govt. of India : Annual Report, Ministry of Rural Development, 1992-93.
7. Ibid.
8. Rajagopal : Status of Rural Marketing, Background Material for the Workshop on DSMS, July 22-24, 1991, NIRD, Hyderabad.
9. Rajagopal : Managing Rural Business : Quest for Approach, Economic Times, Mid-week Review, April 23, 1993.
10. Rajagopal : Administrative Arrangements for Rural Marketing Report, National Institute of Rural Development, Hyderabad, 1993.

3

Institutional Linkages

The planning for credit linked business development in rural enterprises assisted under various rural development programmes is attempetd in some districts of the state on pilot basis through the individual firm's linkages, cooperatives and DSMS. The foregoing text discusses the organisational and functional patterns of different types of credit - marketing linkages established in the Warangal and Khammam districts of the state in ISB sector of IRDP. The present paper attempts to analyse the organisational and functional pattern of integrated linkages comprising credit, training, production and marketing of the selected rural industries products in the Warangal and Khammam districts of Andhra Pradesh.

Integrated Linkages in Rural Enterprises

The backward and forward linkages are very essential for any firm to attain a good economic status. It is an issue of high priority in rural enterprises to make them sustainable in the market competition through an institutional patronage at the take off stage of the firm. The credit, input supply, production technology, post production extension services and marketing assistance form the core of integrated linkages in rural entrepreneurial firms[1]. It has been found that pottery, handloom weaving, leaf plate making, brassware, kalamkari [handloom printing], bamboo basketry and carpet weaving industry are brought into the integrated linkage network assessing methodologically the resource potential and the business opportunities in the region.

Linkages in Individual Firms

Pottery is one of the traditionally regarded industries comprising 12.97 per cent of the total rural workforce engaged in rural industries in the Warangal district. The entrepreneurs of this trade have been provided financial assistance under the IRDP and efforts are being made to pull-up their economic conditions from below the poverty line by organising them into informal groups. This has helped the potters in augmenting their production level and enhancing the scope of marketing.

The study was conducted in the Elland a village of Waradanapet Mandal of Warangal district where the potters guild involved actively in production and the DRDA in providing the marketing support. In all, 24 beneficiaries were selected for building the information base about the impact of post-credit linkages on their production, incremental income and repayment status. It was observed during the study the potters work 220 days on an average per annum. The peak season for the trade will be during February-June. However, the slack season remains for three months during rains commencing from July to September. The specialisation of the potters is found in the production and marketing of 'Ranjans'— a clay pot used as poor man's water cooler and refrigerator. It is useful for cooling the water, keeping vegetables and cooked stuff for 9 to 12 hours. It maintains the temperature between 2 to 6 degrees of centegrade subject to placement at properly ventilated room. The potters have been provided subsidised loan as working capital, besides the assets which have been supplied by the State Khadi and Village Industries Board. The status of borrowings from different sources and the utilisation ratio is exhibited in Table 3.1.

Table 3.1: Financial Assistance and Utilisation

Borrowing Limit [Rs]	*Organi-sation*	*Number of Beneficiaries*	*Extent of Utilisation [%]*	*Purpose*
1000 - 4000	KVIB	06	100	Assets
4000 - 8000	DRDA	24	63. 41	Working Capital

The improved potters' wheels have been provided by the KVIB to the beneficiaries in kind in addition to the loan under IRDP. The working capital provided by DRDA is used to the extent of 63.41 per cent by the beneficiaries since 1989-90. The production rate of Ranjans is found to be high in veiw of the market price as compared to the ordinary clay pots. The working capital is used in procuring the rice bran, saw dust and clay of specific nature which are the principal raw materials for manufacturing the 'Ranjans'. The clay is taken from an identified field and Rs. 2000 is paid as lease rent to the land owner per annum sharing jointly by all the beneficiaries. The economics of 'Ranjans' manufactured per month is exhibited in Table 3.2.

Table 3.2: Economics of Pottery

[Rs per month]

Production Span	*Quantity Produced*	*Cost of Produc-ion*	*Price*		*Value Realised*
			Market	*Contract*	
November-January	180	108	22	09	1628
February-June	300	180	30	08	2400

The data shows that the though the price for the Ranjans in the open market is 76.33 per cent higher than the price offered by the contractors, the potters intend to sell through contractors only. The major incentive which the potters get in channelising the product through the contractors is that there will be no transportation cost and transit loss incured on part of the entreprepeures. The transportation cost accounts for Rs 11 per 100 units for a distance of 25 kilometres and the transit loss would be around 2.81 per cent of the gross product value[2].

The DRDA has provided extension services in terms of skill development, product designing and the marketing support for fine pottery and artistic products through the All India Handicrafts Board. The marketing of such artistic pottery was linked with the Kaktiya Festival organised every year at the district headquarters. Some of these products were also displayed in the PRAGATI EMPORIUM organised by the DSMS in association with the DRDA the district. However, these institutional channels could not delink the middlemen from the pottery trade and thus the common channel for marketing of potter's products in bulk rests with the contractors. The Diagram 3.1 depicts the path of backward and forward linkages in the pottery enterprises.

The beneficiaries earn Rs 3100 per annum on an average and

the rate of repayment is 30.91 per cent of the income earned. It was found that out of the selected sample 04 beneficiaries were selected for the trade fares as stated in the pre-text and earned Rs 3000 net income on an average. However, such opportunities are

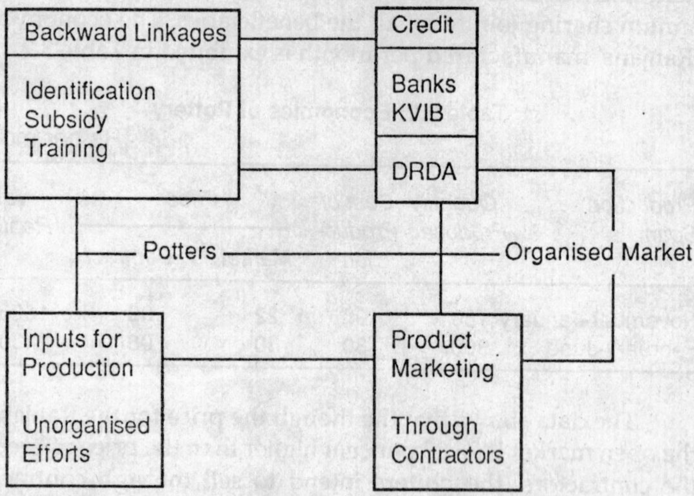

Diagram 3.1: Inflow and Outflow of Rural Products

not regular phenomenon for all the entrepreneurs engaged in the trade. In the Kakatiya Festival and Agricultural Exhibition held in the district during 1992-93, the DRDA facilitated 150 beneficiaries from all trades to participate. The lodge and boarding has been provided free to the participating artisans by the DRDA for all such exhibitions organised within the district. The travel and other logistic support is given to the selected artisans who attend the fairs and festivals out side the district or state by the agency.

The product improvement is one of the major requirements for widening the scope of marketing and augmenting the potential of income generation. The training for skill development has been provided by the All India Handicrafts Board to the potters which was liasoned by the DRDA authorities. It had shown an impact on the incremental income and also improved the repayment capacity of beneficiaries as exhibited in the Table 3.3.

Table 3.3: Impact of Entrepreneurship Development on REFs

Pre-training Economy			*Post-training Economy*		
Income Level		*Repayment [%]*	*Income Level*		*Repayment [%]*
I	*II*		*I*	*II*	
10 [41.67]	14 [58.33]	29.74	07 [29.17]	17 [70.83]	32.09

Level I = 1200-3600 per annum
Level II= 3601-5000 per annum
Figures in parantheses indicate percentage to total sample size.

The data shows that after participation in the skill development training, provided for quality upgradation and contemporary pottery designs, 21.43 per cent beneficiaries shifted to the higher income bracket of Rs. 3601-5000 per annum. The incremental shift in their income level has also increased their repayment potential by 7.90 per cent per annum. Such development indicates the possitive impact of backward and forward linkages on economic change in the rural industries. However, the setting of effective credit-marketing linkage has to be achieved through better coordination with the sectoral departments and the financing institutions.

The basic dichotomy which often intercepts the marketing decisions of artisans is the direct sales to the consumers verses the intermediate channel. The institutional attempt to promote the direct sales through the Pragati Emporium was not uphailed by the artisans as it was on the consignment basis. The fine and artistic clay products do not possess the local demand though the prices are attractive in the markets located out side the district. The artisans opined that the trade protection is required at the initial stages to expand the business opportunities and market. The Andhra Pradesh Handicrafts Development Corporation may be linked with the marketing of products of rural entrepreneurs assisted under various development programmes. The Diagram 3.2 shows the model for setting up such linkages with state level corporations which can explore the inter-state and export markets for the improved products of local artisans.

The coordinated model exhibits that the DRDA has to assume a major role in establishing a linkage network liasoning with financing and marketing agencies. The indent for specific products may be put to the DRDA to assemble the products from the artisans for channelising through the marketing agency. The Emporium organised by DSMS under the patronage of DRDA may take-up this task of liasoning with the marketing agency of higher order. The loan repayment can be deducted at the source and regularised by remitting the collection to the concerned financial institution for adjustment against the borrowings of the beneficiaries. This would also facilitate the financing institutions to improve their recovery status. In all, such coordinated model will function effectively and improve the economic condition of the firm by providing assured credit and business opportunities in the competitive market environment.

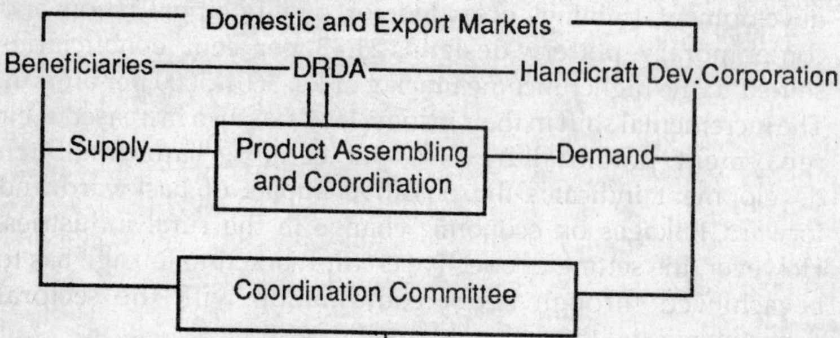

Banks	DRDA	Handicrafts	Beneficiary
Resources Income and Repayment Assessment Deduction at Source	Selection Training Inputs Output Channelising	Market Demand Supply Orders Negotiating Price Payments	High Quality Placing Demand Reinvestment Bargaining

Diagram 3.2: Model for Business Linked Development Planning

Linkages in Rural Development Cooperatives

Organising IRDP beneficiaries in formal groups with a legal status for quality production, higher investment and better marketing opportunities has been a recent concept in rural development. The formal groups are registered as trusts or cooperative societies. The major advantage of such group dynamism is streching the rural - urban product markets and the bargaining power for financial assistance as well as for the better price of the product[3]. It is observed that group dynamics in marketing develops the logistics in various business activities. The group activities are instrumental to build-up linkages in the rural enterprises. The experiment of organising a weavers cooperative society of IRDP beneficiaries in Warangal district has projected many dimensions of effective backward and forward linkages followed in a institutional approach.

The concept of weavers organisation was moved among the individual weavers assisted under IRDP in the district with an intention to have a secured wage earning provided by the patronaged institute. The Andhra Pradesh Cooperative Handloom Federation has been conceived as mother unit for employment generation. In all, 60 weavers were identified initially for providing assistance under IRDP. The infrastructure for working at a common place has been created by the DRDA. In terms of assest each weaver has been provided with a loom costing Rs. 3300 of which 10 per cent cost was met by the beneficiaries. The common workshed has been constructed by the DRDA using the earmarked funds for infrastructure in IRDP. The cooperative society was existing in the village prior to rendering the financial assistance to the IRDP beneficiaries. The IRDP beneficiaries have been inducted in this cooperative since 1987-88 and their membership is found increasing in the subsequent years. The Table 3.4 exhibits the growth of membership of IRDP beneficiaries during the period 1987-91. The data reveals that the IRDP beneficiaries contribute 18.14 per cent to the total membership. A major advantage of the cooperative membership is observed in negotiating an assured marketing linkage with the Andhra Pradesh Cooperative Handloom Weavers Society [APCO], an 'APEX'cooperative organisation in the state. The APCO supplies the required quantity of yarn to the members of the society for weaving the specified quantity of cloth. The finished clothes are procured by APCO at the rate of Rs. 3 per metre for cotton and Rs. 5 per metre for the polyster cloth. Such backward and forward linkages provide the weavers regular employment and income. The women members are engaged in the yarn reeling activity and work 270 days per year on an average. Table 3.5 shows the activity-wise income earned by the beneficiaries in the society.

Table 3.4: Membership of IRDP Beneficiaries

Year	Membership		
	IRDP	Other	Total
1987-88	25	165	190
1989-90	19	205	224
1990-91	43 [30]	237	280

Figures in Parantheses indicate women members.

Table 3.5: Activity-wise Income Generation

Activity	Wage Rate [Rs/mt]	Quantity Produced [mts/month]	Income Generated [Rs/month]
Cotton Weaving	3.00	150	450.00
Polyster Weaving	5.00	110	550.00
Yarn Reeling [per cone]	5.00	60	300.00

The data shows that women workers earn Rs 2700 per annum and the weavers generate income of Rs 6000 per annum on an average. The payment for the procured cloth from the weavers is made after 150 days by APCO. Though the cloth is not procured from the weavers on the consignment basis by APCO, the delay in payments is found to be a procedural delay. The apex society provides linkages to the primary cooperative society as an unit. However the individual weavers are not provided any support by APCO. The functional pattern of backward and forward linkages in weaving trade is exhibited in the Diagram 3.3.

The IRDP beneficiaries, who are members of the cooperative society are also eligible to get supplementary credit

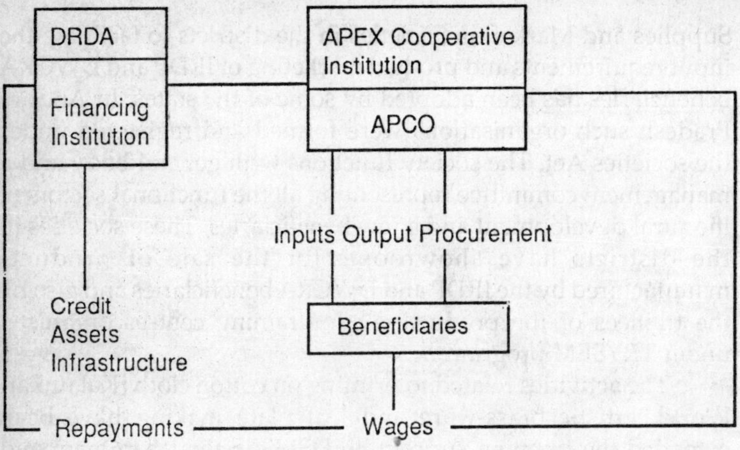

Digram 3.3: Coordination Path of Link Institution

from the District Central Cooperative Bank subject to the liquidation of loan drawn under IRDP. It was found that the society has achieved sustainable group dynamics and can resist to the short run market changes. However, reveiwing the overall system of linkages a fundamental question emerges that how long the patronage of APCO is required ? The whole functional pattern caters more significantly the employment needs of the weavers than scope for generating incremental income. Such institutional patronage in the long run may develop dependency of the weavers on the 'apex' institution and limit the prospects for their products in the open market, if the production is conceived by the society on its own resources. However a primary weavers cooperative society entering into an open market economy with full autonomy seems to be a far cry[4].

Linkages with District Supply and Marketing Society

The arrangements for making the assured supply of inputs at regular intervals and rendering the marketing support for the products manufactured by the rural entreprises assisted under rural development programmes was a debated since the inception of production oriented programmes like IRDP, DWCRA etc. The policy guidelines for organising the District

Supplies and Marketing Societies in the districts to facilitate the input requirements and product marketing of IRDP and DWCRA beneficiaries has been adopted by some of the states. In Andhra Pradesh such organisations were formed and registered under the societies Act. The society functions with general body and a management committee representing all the functional sectors of the rural development and a few beneficiaries. These societies in the districts have showrooms for the sale of products manufactured by the IRDP and DWCRA beneficiaries and also by the trainees of the production-cum-training centres organised under TRYSEM programme.

The activities related to printing on cotton cloth [Kalamkari Work], artistic brass-ware and leaf plate making have been extended the creeping support by DSMS in the Khammam and Warangal districts of Andhra Pradesh. These societies with their show-rooms have been organised in December 1991 and June 1993 respectively, specifying the brands in particular. The product brands of DSMS at Warangal is named PRAGATI and GRAMSHRI at Khammam. The beneficiaries engaged in the above trade are being assisted for getting the required inputs for uninterrupted production through the society. The inputs provided to the beneficiaries through the society costs 2.76 per cent less that the market price and the products manufactured with the inputs are inturn procured by the society for sales through their show-rooms. Table 3.6 exhibits the sales trend of DSMS show-rooms in both the districts.

Table 3.6: Marketing of Rural Products through DSMS [Pragati: 1992-93] [Amount in '000 Rs]

Major Items	*Procurement per annum*	*Sales*	
		Average per month	*Gross per annum*
Artistic Brassware	43.26	4.44	53.30
Leather Goods	68.91	6.02	72.31
Handloom Clothes	110.00	10.11	121.34

The data reveals that the sales performance in the Pragati showroom is not even reached the break even point as the DSMS has been established on the policy lines of Government of India with an outlay of Rs 10 lakhs to be utilised in the period of three years. Accordingly an amount of Rs 1. 80 lakhs is earmarked towards the rent, infrastructure and sales emporium, Rs. 40 thousands is provisioned for the purchase of samples and a seed capital of Rs 5.0 lakhs from the DRDA funds to run the society. The subsidy towards the managerial costs, furnitures and fixtures have been evenly distributed for the three years period at the rate of 33.33 per cent which is being provided by the central government[5]. However, reviewing at the performance of the society in the open market it can also apply take soft loans from the SIDBI etc. for business expansion.

It is found during the study that the DSMS is under full patronage and required to perform the business above the break even point for a minimum period of three years soon after it starts functioning on its own resources.

Inter-Institution Linkages

The marketing institutional linkage for the input supply and marketing assistance to the beneficiaries of various production oriented rural development programmes like IRDP, DWCRA etc has been urged by the planners since long. It could not take an uniformal shape over the decade of launching IRDP due the administrative constraints in many states. The Seventh Five Year Plan also envisaged the need for an organisation to cater the needs of inputs and output marketing in the unorganised sector of rural industries substantially glutted with the IRDP and DWCRA beneficiaries. However, it was observed that the Goa was the only state which realised the need for institutional linkage in such unorganised rural sector and successfully operationalised the tie-up arrangements between the District Rural Development Agency and the Goa handicrafts Rural and Small Scale Industries Development Corporation (GHRSSIDC)[6]. The foregoing text describes the institutional linkage in administering the rural marketing in the North District of the Goa state.

Marketing is a process which involves reactions of various interlinking factors consisting of use of resources to the approaches for maximising/profit within a given framework of market economy. The overall perfcrmance and behaviour of these inter-linkages form a system of product marketing. In any of such system investment, production and marketing each govern a set of functions which determine the efficiency of the overall marketing system. The Diagram 3.4 exhibits the functional components of the rural marketing system. The

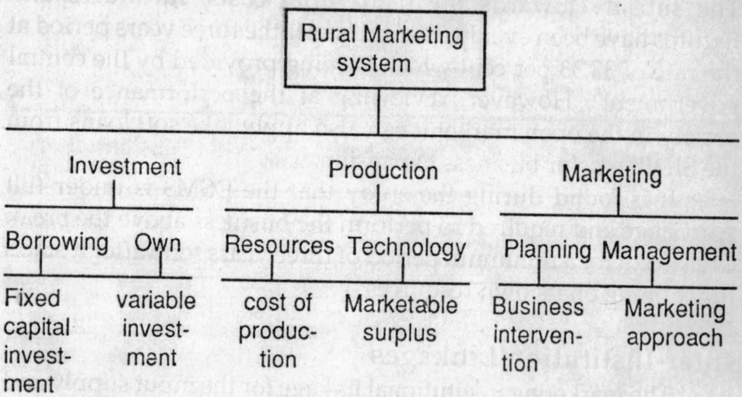

Digram 3.4: Conponents of Rural Marketing System

investment on resource utilization for production largely depends on the source of finance available with rural intrepreneurial firms (REF). The investment for production is a function of cost, technology and quality parametres, which determines the production potential, marketable surplus etc. The marketing is an important function to be performed for the wider absorption of marketable surplus with an objective of large consumer coverage and profit maximisation to the best possible extent. It is observed that REFs stress on minimising the risk because of many economic limitations, than maximising profit. The basic characteristics of REFs in context to social, economic, technological and business aspects is exhibited in Table 3.7. It can be seen from the above description that the rural business is carried out by REF's in isolation where they lack in competitive environment and business strategies. These are some of the economic lapses that affect the overall business efficiency of REF's in general and of the entrepreneurs lying below poverty line who sought financial assistance under IRDP/DWARA in particular. The integration of these characteristics form the marketing system in rural areas. The foregoing text discusses in detail the various dimensions of marketing approaches, production system and the extension strategies followed to promote the REF's assisted under IRDP/DWCRA programmes.

Table 3.7: Basic Characteristics of REFs

Social	*Economic*	*Technological*	*Business*
Casts and area bound	Low investment	Traditional skills	Small marketable surplus
Resistant to urban intervention for development	Low production	Low level of adoption of improved technology	No stocking
Traditional values in occupation	Infrastructural problems	Labour intensive technology preferable	One man enterprise
Family oriented.	Low earnings	Financial handicaps for absorption of new technology	Low risk taking ability
	Less exposure to external economics		Low profit
			Pricing, distribution and product promotion problems

It is evident from the discussion in the pre-text that in rural economy production and marketing are complementary to each other. The production and investment pattern in ISB sector determines the kind of product to be manufactured, its design and quality, local market for the product and forward market for inter-district and inter-state trade, with reference to rural industrial products. It can be stated that the production system is one of the important components in the life cycle of a firm for establishing the trade practice in rural areas. The production of need based commodities in rural areas always create large markets. It is observed during the study that the basketry and brick making trades cater the industrial and constructional needs of the district to a large extent, and are also suplied to the neighbouring districts in the state. However, the commodities produced in other trades have limited market within the district.

Input Management

It is an important process in the overall economy of a rural entrepreneurial firm. The consumer behaviour and market potential largely depend on the quality and quantity of the production. These two factors have various other determinents like infrastructure, technology, knowledge attitude and practising ability (KAP) etc. The production infrastructure consists of availability of raw material, plant and mechinery, energy and the production technology. In all, it was found except capital intensive machineries, the rural entrepreneurial firms had all required infrastructure for production. The raw material was locally available and the entrepreneurs had direct trade links with the private businessmen.

Production System

The production system in REFs engaged in non-form sector largely depend on the network of backward linkages consisting of credit, product designing, storage, inputs, technology etc. It has been observed during the study that in the fibre, Bamboo and cane industries, the production level is still traditional. However, GHRSSIDC has provided considerable awareness on product designing and technology use to increase the, production and marketability. There is a close coherance between these linkages and setting up business in a competitive environment. These factors determine the production system of REFs to a considerable extent.

Market Hierarchy

In the study region for marketing of the products of REFs, the three tier marketing system exists. In this structure the district market which is also the market located at state capital Panaji, town markets and village markets constitute in an ascending order of hierarchy. There are 8 town markets in the district, including one at the state capital. These town markets serve as growth centres and cater the financial and commercial needs of the village markets located in their hinterland to a large extent.

The intermediaries consisting of middlemen and contractors operate from the town markets while the itinerant traders function from a central village which is linked to weekly markets. The middlemen and contractors attend the village markets where specific commodities are brought by the entrepreneures for sale like handicrafts, fibre products, processed food items, readymade garments sea-shell products etc. The itinerant traders visit the weekly markets of their surrounding round the week and procure the products. The weekly markets are mainly the assembling centres for the commodities of hinterland whereas these products are graded in town markets. In terms of functional activities these markets can be grouped into three distinct categories-the first, second and third order markets as terminal, secondary and primary markets. There is one market of first order located in district headquarter and its main function is performing inter district and inter-state transactions marketing and financing marketing agents operating in second and third order markets. Since this district is bordering to Maharashtra state, some commodities like sea-shell products, handicrafts, fibre and soft toy items etc are also bought by the traders of the neighbouring districts of Maharashtra state in small quantity. The bamboo baskets produced in the district have a local market and is largely used for the mining and querrying activities. Some of the bamboo articles manufactured by the IRDP beneficiaries is supplied to the emporia of GHRSSIDC and some retail outlets owned by the private traders at the places of tourists attraction.

The second order markets are located in the block head-quarters. The products procured by the commission agents and contractors, in weekly markets is graded in these markets and priced accordingly. The itinerant traders who visit the weekly markets and procure products are also sold to commission agents and graded properly. Sometimes the commission agents in turn finance the itinerant traders to procure and assemble the products from weekly markets. The contractors select the cluster of entrepreneurs proffessionally engaged in particular trade and place order in bulk. Such instances are observed with regard to readymade garments, handicrafts, fibre and bamboo products. The IRDP beneficiaries use such channel for ready made garments and handicrafts in Tiswadi block and for bamboo products in Perne and Sattari blocks. One of the main advantages in this channel is that an entrepreneur gets a ready market for the mandays utilised in production. However, the prices are not fixed at higher level because of limited options and bargaining.

The markets held periodically in the villages are the third order markets in the existing hierarchichal structure of markets in the district. These markets are frequently visited by the itinerant traders. These markets are generally of mixed type providing almost all necessary requirements of the rural people. The network of third order markets brings the rural producers and traders close to each other on a common economic platform. These markets mainly serve as an assembling centre for the products, intended for inter and intra-district trade. However a small amount of commodities are sold locally for consumption.

Hierarchical Inter-Relationship

The market hierarchy in the district has a pyramidical structure with the first order market at the top, second order markets in the middle and the third order markets at the bottom. Thus, the functional integration among these market orders is vertical. The procurement of commodities is carried in large quantities in the second order market of which a part of stock is mobilised within the district and the rest through first order market for inter-district trade. The credit mobilisation is top-down approach from first order market to second and third order markets. The town markets serve as a distribution centre for the products in their hinterland. The quality control and grading of products is largely done in these market centres. Another important character of town markets which are in second order of market hierarchy, also to serve as a growth centre catering the basic needs of the villages of the hinterland. The demand for inter-district marketing of specific commodities percolates through the town markets. The merchants located in district market provide infrastructure facilities like transport, storage, electricity, insurance etc. to the traders in town markets for promoting supplies. In turn, the traders based in town markets extend such support to limited itinerant traders who procure products from village markets. These are the important functions that establish the market linkages in the existing hierarchy in the district. Such inter-linkages of markets help in systematic flow of goods and services from village market to district market and vice-versa.

Trade Channels

In general, for the procurement of rural industrial products there are five trade channels operating in the district, which involve itinerant traders, middleman, contractors, retailers and marketing institution like GHRSSIDC with sales counters and emporia. The marketing efficiency of these channels depends on various factors such as producer's share in consumer's rupee, distribution of marketing margin, marketing cost, price variation and the propensity of demand for the product etc. Besides, the private marketing channels, the corporation helps the IRDP beneficiaries to market their products through its distinguished outlets. The corporation is very selective in procurement and sales of entrepreneurial products manufactured by the beneficiaries. The corporation prefers to buy only demand oriented products with specific design and quality. The GHRSSIDC also procures from the entrepreneurs assisted other than IRDP/DWCRA in the district. To ensure quality of the products the corporation provides training to the artisans in some of the important trades like pottery through its training centre at Bicholim. The popular channel among the other existing in rural areas is the itinerants trader followed by retailer and consumer. However for marketing of rural products in urban areas the channel linking middleman, wholesaler and retailer is commonly used. The above two channels are popular among non-institution marketing outlets in the district. The linkage of RDA and GHRSSIDC in marketing of REFs products constitute the institutional network. Many times the GHRSSIDC gets into the business ties directly with the artisans and negotiates the deal with in the set parameters of the corporation viz. quantity, quality, design and pricing. The scope of contractors is observed in some inter-state export potential products such as sea-shell articles, fibre bamboo and cane products etc. However the contractors do not generally channelise their product within the state markets.

Trade Practice

As discussed in the pre-text, there are many channels involved in procurement and marketing of products of REFs in the study region It is observed during the study that the beneficiaries select the channel for marketing based on the potentiality of the product. For instance, the bamboo and cane products of course quality viz. storage bins, mats etc. one sold either directly to the consumer or to the itinerant traders who in turn sell them in different village markets. Since the sea-shell, fibre and handicrafts have underscope of marketing within and outside the state, it is sold through the contractors, middleman and to some extent GHRSSIDC. The processed food items, pottery, readymade garments etc. have substantial local market and so are marketed through the itinerant traders, GHRSSIDC and to large extent directly to the consumers. The Table 3.8 exhibits the marketing practices adopted in sale of different kinds of products.

Table 3.8: Product Movement Through Different Channels

(Value in per cent)

Sl. No.	*Trades/Channel*	*I*	*II*	*III*	*IV*	*V*	*VI*	*Total Respon-dents*
1.	Procesed food industry	12. 82	14.07	-	10. 18	62. 93	-	23 (100)
2.	Sea-shell industry	—	—	22. 55	22. 67	6. 74	48.04	11 (100)
3.	Soft toys & Handicrafts	—	20. 98	7. 31	19. 85	10. 11	41. 75	12 (100)
4.	Pottery	21. 32	—	—	4.06	74. 62	—	15 (100)
5.	Bamboo & cane Industry	5. 73	—	2. 16	9. 87	58. 33	23. 41	50 (100)
6.	Fibre Industry	—	11. 35	20. 81	6. 24	15. 72	45. 88	15 (100)
7.	Readymade Garments	12.04	10. 23	—	11. 93	26. 74	39.06	29 (100)

Channel = I = itinerant trader, II= Wholesaler, III= Contractors, IV = GHRSSIDC, V = Director, VI = Exhibition

The data reveals that the beneficiaries largely prefer to sell the products directly to the consumers. However, the exhibitions organised by the GHRSSIDC, RDA and other government departments of the state provide scope for marketing the products in sea-shell, handicrafts, fine bamboo, fibre and readymade garments industries. In all, above 39.79 per cent of total value of sales is contributed by such exhibitions to the artisans. It has been observed during the study that the REFs have quick turnover of stock in some of trades which are engaged in manufacturing of consumable items such as processed food products, pottery and readymade garments. There is an immediate local market for such products and the entrepreneurs need not necessarily wait for the consignment orders from the contractors, wholesalers or GHRSSIDC authorities. However for the sea-shell, fibre, handicrafts and fine bamboo products, the entrepreneurs have to wait for the supply orders from the GHRSSIDC or other channels. These products are despatched to the consignee traders within 45 days on an average. The Table 3.9 depicts the time taken for production and supplies to different channels by the REFs engaged in various trades.

Table 3.9: Turnover Span in Different Trades

Sl. No.	*Trades*	*Value of Supplier order (Rs.)*	*Type of commodity*	*Production time***	*Time taken for Despatching consignment In different channels*		
					I	*II*	*III*
1.	Sea shell Product	20, 000	Certain & toys	65	03	03	09
2.	Handicrafts	6, 700	Variety	90	02	03	07
3.	Fibre Products	10, 000	Bags of Different size	110	05	05	07
4.	Readymade Garments	12, 765	Shorts & Vests	60	07	02	03
5.	Fine Bamboo Products	5, 400	Bamboo Garments	78	05	03	07

* Channels code : I = contractors, II = Wholesalers and III = GHRSSIDC.

** Time in Mandays.

The time taken for despatching the consignment indicates the average mandays required for grading, packaging and transportation of the products. The contractors and wholesalers paid the amount immediately on receipt of the consignment. So the entrepreneurs met the transportation charges and delivered the indented quantity of goods immediately. In case of supply orders by GHRSSIDC, the transport is provided by the corporation. The delay is thus, caused in supplying the products to the corporation. It has been highlighted in some of the similar studies conducted in different parts of the country that there would be higher inclination of entrepreneurs towards private trade channels due to social and economic tie-ups. Such association is built-up for selecting the obligations of traders for marketing and social help. However such kind of attitude was not found among the artisans in the study area. It can be seen from the Table 3.9 that large number of entrepreneurs prefer to sell the product directly rather than the private or institutional channels. In all, the order of preference for marketing channel is found to be 25.2% for private traders, 23.9% for contractors, 1.3% for corporative organisations, 1.9% for GHRSSIDC and 47.8% for direct sales to the consumers. There are many reasons for selling the products through non-institutional channels. Of these some are exhibited in Table 3.10.

Table 3.10: Preference Parameters for Marketing Channels

Sl. No.	*Parameter*	*Frequency (Response)*	*Percentage for Total*
1.	Satisfactory Price	92	59.4
2.	Graded Price	9	5.8
3.	Timely Payment	18	11.6
4.	Bulk Procurement Orders	20	12.9
5.	Prompt Procurement	16	10.3
		155	100.00

The price spread or the cost of marketing has an important consideration in pricing and profit mechanisms. The price spread includes the cost incurred towards transportation, storage, middlemen's margin, communication etc. in mobilising the product for sale in the market though the opted channel of marketing. The Table 3.11 exhibits the price spread in different constitutents and their respective shares.

Table 3.11: Price Spread* in Different Trades

Sl. No.	Traaes	Total cost of marketing (Rs/Month)	Price Spread (in per cent)			
			Trans-port	Storage	Middle-men's margin	Inci-den-tal char-ges
1.	Processed Food Industry	155.68	20.94	6.23	24.55	48.28
2.	Sea Shell Industry	261.72	39.61	4.02	36.97	19.4
3.	Soft Toys & Handicrafts	145.09	28.61	4.93	19.65	46.81
4.	Pottery	157.64	14.05	1.96	—	83.99
5.	Bamboo and Cane Industry	88.37	26.17	—	21.84	51.99
6.	Fibre Industry	93.18	36.66	8.01	15.62	39.71
7.	Readymade Garments	192.65	42.04	—	12.36	45.6

* Average to the total sample size.

The data indicates that in marketing of the products of REFs incidental charges have major share in the price spread followed by the transportation cost. The share of middlemen's margin in price spread consists of 26.2 per cent on an average. It is found during the study that the entrepreneurs practically do not spread any amount in product storage for the reasons: (i) they try to sell items immediately (ii) The products are stored at their own house or sametimes in shared accommodation and (iii) the quantity of products manufactured is small to store for long run. Since the level of production is low in REFs they require quick recycling of money for consumption and further investment, under such circumstances, the entrepreneurs try to sell the products immediately without storing them for better market gain. The private traders initially offer low prices for the products of REFs. However, the price is finally settled through bargaining and negotiations. It has been observed during the study that the entrepreneurs engaged in manufacturing sea shell, bamboo and cane, readymade garments and fibre products have better bargaining power because of availability of alternative channels of marketing. However, the entrepreneurs of other trades do not enter into such bargains and sell the products at the dictated prices of traders.

Retailing Practice

Retailing has been defined as one of the branches of Marketing Science, This segment is relatively complex than wholesaling and trade contracting as it has a fragmented scope of sales with more generalistic aproach. The retail stores are not specialised in particular commodity. However the dealership is different than retailing the commodities in general economic sense. Retailing in entrepreneur himself acts as retailer in many occasions. The retail transactions, infact provide feedback of consumers behaviours and the propensity of product movement in the market. Thus, it is an important segment to be studied indepth to facilitate the marketing management concept at base line. Keeping these facts in view, the study on retailing products brought out through IRDP and DWCRA programmes has been thought of.

The common retail outlets in the region are (i) periodic markets and (ii) the emopria of GHRSSIDC. In the periodic markets the rural producers sell their produce while the traders, who assemble the products from different places in the state perform comparatively larger scale of trade. The basic characteristics identified during the study about the rural producer - sellers and traders are exhibited in Table 3.12. The traders possess an itinerant character which keep them mobile all through the six days of a week to attend the periodic markets for selling and procuring the potential products grown and manufactured in respective hinterlands. This particular character enhances the scope of marketing. The main objective of producer-seller is in acquire money for immediate consumption than investment in business. Such conditions encourage professional traders business morale and in long run they dominate the market operations.

The weekly transactions of producer-seller are low as compared to the professional traders due to occasional attendance in the market and restricted mobility. The producers also often act as retailers and attend the local markets held periodically. However, it is observed that their frequency to visit the markets in the hinterland is lower as compared to the professional traders due to the predominent reason of transport. Thus, the value of sales realisation for producers is also low. The Table 3.13 exhibits the transaction status of rural products by category of traders.

Table 3.12: Characteristics of Retailers

Sl.	Indicators	Producer seller	Professional Retailer
1.	Nature & scope	Confined for own products	Liberal to all products having potential market
2.	Market attendance	Own Village	All Neighbouring markets
3.	Goods Supplied	Own product	Imported, regionally produced, along with fruits and vegetables
4.	Stock	None	Small but assorted
5.	Finance	Practically nil	Relatively more for procurement and transportation
6.	Labour input	One - man enterprise	Family enterprise
7.	Risk	Low	High
8.	Economic Integration	Absent	Significant with forward markets
9.	Social Integration	High	High
10.	Profit	Subsistance	Relatively more
11.	Main motto	Money for immediate consumption	Survival and expansion of business

Table 3.13: Gross Sales Realisation in Retailing

(Values in Rs. /Week)

Sl. No.	Products	Producer-seller	Professional traders
1.	Processed food	89.64 (1)	492.75 (4)
2.	Bamboo and Cane Products	38.00 (2)	114.55 (5)
3.	Sea-shell	93.75 (1)	538.30 (6)
4.	Readymade garments	147.34 (2)	881.50 (6)
5.	Fibre Products	65.55 (1)	109. 25 (4)
6.	Pottery	82.65 (1)	64.35 (1)
7.	Lace and embroidery	102.80 (1)	596.80 (3)

Figures in parentheses indicate number of markets attended.

The margin of profit in retail trading is higher than the

wholesalers. However, at the same time the producers' price in consumer's rupee seems to be lower. The Table 3.14 shows the extent of marketing margin earned by the retailers over the producers' price.

Table 3.14: Producer's Price in Consumers' Rupee

	Processed food	*Ready-made garments*	*Sea shell products*
Producers' price (Pp)	300.00	2200.00	1500.00
Wholesaler's price (Wp)	318.00	2260.00	1775.00
Retailer's price (Rp)	350.00	2500.00	2250.00
Weighted average Price (Pwrp)	338.48	2452.00	2075.83
Producers' share in Consumers' rupee (%) (pp - Pwrp x 100)	88.63	89.72	72.29

* For computation specifications see Appendix 1.

It may be seen from the table that the retailers earning in ready made garments and processed food are more as compared to other products. It may be due to two basic characteristics of the product (i) durability and (ii) essential nature. The retailers earn higher margin in the shell-curtains as it is a conspicuous item and has greater circulation in market as compared to other products. The Table reveals that 11.37, 10.28 and 27.71 per cent amount of the consumers' price is distributed as marketing margin among the channels involved in marketing of processed food, ready-made garment and sea-shell products respectively.

It has been observed that shorter the chain of intermediaries, higher is the profit margin for producers. The rural products need institutional channels to maximise their margin. The GHRSSIDC has opened outlet to the Goan craftsmen to market their products through institution. However, the coverage of RDP assisted artisans is comparatively low to the other skilled craftsmen. The corporation is profit oriented and thus largely demand oriented in procurement of rural products. Table 3.15 exhibits the performance of GHRSSIDC in procurement and sales of handicrafts and rural industries products including items selected for the study. The data reveals that the turnover is significant and the procurement sales ratio is also > 1 on an average. The corporation procures the products of goan and non-goan origin for sales through its emporia spread within and outside the state. Of these, the goan products constitute 60.46 per cent of overall procurements made by GHRSSIDC on an average.

Table 3.15: Institutional Support for Marketing of Rural Products

(Value in lakh Rs)

Year	*Market Operations of GHRSSIDC*		*Procure-ment sales Ratio*
	Procurement	*Sales*	
1987-88	6.92	11.56	1 : 1.67
1988-89	11.08	10.73	1 : 1. 11
1989-90	12.66	14.16	1 : 1. 11

The Corporation has presently adopted different procedures for procurement of rural products as stated in Table 3.16. The products which are procured on consignment basis are kept in emporia and exhibition for specific period and payment is made on the quantity and items sold. The remaining entities are returned. The selling prise for such products are fixed on the parity basis of similar products. The regular orders are made taking two major market issues into consideration (i) the product demand and (ii) new launching on trial basis. The products are also sold in exhibitions, by the corporation and also under the banner of the other trade fair authorities. The products sold in exhibition during 1987 and 1989 are worth Rs.1.04 and 0.09 lakhs respectively.

Table 3.16: Institutional Procedures for Product Procurement

Sl. No.	*Procedure*	*Explanation*
1.	Consignment Basis	Payment on sales within specific time or return.
2.	Regular Order	Outright procurement for sales, and on demand by potential buyers.

The Goan craftsmen have three channels of marketing. They are (i) direct to consumer (ii) through wholesalers and (iii) through institution. It was observed that the second channel is more popular in the marketing of rural products, as the product is purchased in bulk by the wholesalers and the craftsmen get money immediately. Though the institutional channel is more profitable and provides stability in product marketing, it does not serve the purpose of craftsmen of getting immediate money. The data shows that 28.61 per cent of total sample craftsmen prefer to sell their products through the corporation. However, they had some established rural products.

The analysis of the all approaches followed in establishing the credit marketing linkage in the rural enterprises seems to be lacking in a well nurtured marketing strategy coordinated with the supporting institutions of the higher order to promte the business. It is not easy to create a potential demand for the product within the district or hinterland as the consumers have the informal knowledge of the product and its value added characteristics. Thus, it is necessary to tap the markets outside the hinterland through consumer awareness approaches.

It is also necessary for the financing agencies to assess the viability of the units from the point of view of the marketability of the products produced and the incremental income generated during the time limit of debt liquidation. The financing agencies may require an feasibilty proposal for such production oriented units. The NABARD may workout the profiles of business linked development in rural enterprises along with their credit potentials.

Planning for Business Linked Development

Institutional credit is one of the important components in the dynamics of rural development. It has been the major source of investment under various rural development programmes. The lending of institutional credit is being supplemented by the government subsidies to the beneficiaries at the grass roots. In the developing countries like India the mobilisation of institutional credit for non-farm economic activities had met substantial credit demand in the rural areas. However, many research and evaluation reports endorsed that the application of credit is not attempted on business logistics and viable propositions. Some observations reveal that lack of inter- and intra-institutional coordination has generated such gulf to a large extent. Thus, credit planning at the district level has high significance in carrying out the true economic objectives in development of activities in rural industries sector.

The administrative system in needs to be re-oriented and efforts to analyse the norms credit plannning for ISB sector. It is necessary to consider the local need for the product proposed to be developed by the unit and the market potential, distribution network and the scope of sustaining the market forces for the product need to be assessed. Thus the developmental plans need to be restructured based on the bottom-up approach.

A detailed exercise need to be done to formulate the Annual Credit Plan for the banks by participation or should we say physical presence of all heads of the department in a district aiming for development projects headed by the District Collector. Alike, any credit planning exercise effective credit planning for the ISB sector has also five critical stages — review of plan performance, potential assessment for the current year, prioritisation, task allocation and monitoring. The efficency of the plan largely depends on the process integration in the above stages. It requires coordination among the economic needs of the people and the sectoral departments assigned with the targets of credit mobilisation. It has been found during the study that the formulation of credit plan for the ISB sector where market economy is to be conisdered for assessment, are largely subject to the arithematic projections and less based on the business logistics. Table 3.17 exhibits the approach followed on some major issues involved in formulation of credit plan.

It is observed that there exists a gulf between the policy and practice at different levels of functionaries. The village level exercises lays the base of the credit plan but is found to be unlogical in many instances as such exercises are largely being subjective and followed by assumptions. The formulation of plan is also not guided properly according to the potential linked development planning manual of NABARD for initial scrutiny of the entries. The reason for lack of logical treatment of the plan document is also a notable drawback at the functionaries of meso level. The assessment of economic potential comprising the viability assessment on the basis of market parametres is not

Table 3.17: Status of Planning for ISB Sector

Clusters/Planning Regions	*Parametre*	*Skill*	*Approach*
Micro/Village	* Need and Potential Assessment	Traditional Local Knowledge	Observation & Conventional perceptions
Meso/Block	* Logistics	Absent	* Individual
	* Economic assessment	Partial	* In consultation bankers
Macro/District	* Pilot Planning & Review	Administrative	* Target oriented * Political considerations
	* Coordination	Pre-fixed Agenda & Administrative Notes	* Heterogenous
	* Monitoring	Statistical reporting	* Sectoral data base

Table 3.18: Activity Scheduling in BLDP

Clusters	*Region*	*Activity*	*Staff*	*Time Schedule*
Micro	Village	Need Assessment and Resource Assessment	VDO Field-Officers	*June-September*
Meso	Block	Prioritisation of Activities ISB sector Preparing Profiles of proposed ventures and estimation of Credit Needs	BDO, Ind. Ext. Officer & Branch Mgr.	*October-Dec.*
Macro	District	Analysing with business logistics geographical alignment, Infrastructure Assessment and Plan finalisation	DRDA, DIC, LBO and NABARD	*January-March*

scientifically carried out and is based on the statistical progressions of the previous plan documents. The target oriented approach makes the plan implementation a mandatory than a logical development concept. The district administration which is the nodle agency for integrated development in the district often is wrapped with the confusion of allocating the sectoral financial targets.

However, this exercise in due course of time becomes leads to heterogenity in implementation as they are carried out by the sectoral department with their own administrative pattern. Hence, application of such system in credit planning generates gaps in plan implementation, monitoring and evaluation.

It is required that the planning for ISB sector has to be carried out in a more scientific manner as it is subject to the open market conditions. Table 3.18 exhibits the schematic pattern of time and work management in formulating the credit plan within the given administrative network. Obviously, with this kind of clear-cut guidelines from the district the banker will widen his vision while formulating the credit plan for ISB sector with better prospect for the employment, income generation for the beneficiary as well as prescribing a secured repayment of the loan to safeguard the interest of the bank.

References

1. Rajagopal : Linkages in IRDP : Lessons from States, Kurukshetra, April, 1991.
2. For similar findings see Rajagopal : Rural Marketing in India: Empirical Studies from Madhya Pradesh, Rennaissance Publishing House, Delhi, 1989.
3. Shah Tushar : Cooperatives and Rural Development, IRMA Seminar Paper, IRMA, Anand, 1991.
4. Rajagopal : Perspectives of Member Control in Cooperatives: A Study of Fruits and Vegetables Cooperatives, IRMA, 1992
5. Govt. of India : Draft DSMS Scheme, Department of Rural Development, Official Communication, New Delhi, 1991.
6. Rajagopal : Input Supply and Marketing Assistance to IRDP Beneficiaries: A Study of Goa State, Report. National Institute of Rural Development, Hyderabad, 1993.

4

Marketing Through Cooperatives

The Concept

The production activities in farm and non-farm sector are largely concentrated in rural areas in India and are being regarded as a feeder source for the processing industries and markets located in urban areas. But the majority of farmers and entrepreneurs are unorganised and individually powerless against the market forces. The people's participation was encouraged by political groups during pre-independence period to claim for their economic rights. Later various organisation, with view to protect their interest have been initiated during post independence period by government and non-government organisation (NGOs). These organisations were regulated under cooperative societies act in subsequent years after independence. By and large, the organisation cooperative institutions in various sectors for production, processing and marketing has been considered as a major attempt against the exploitation by private traders and in developing an efficient alternative marketing channel[1]. However the origin of the marketing cooperatives in India dates back to 1915 when the activities of credit cooperative societies were extended towards marketing of agricultural produce. The strength of cooperative marketing societies in India during 1985 was 5,942 against the number 9,778 in 1955-56. Many societies were closed down due to infrastructural financial and legal problems.

The cooperative processing and marketing societies serving farmers and rural entrepreneurs present diversity in their performance. It has been found at inter and intra-regional level. The cooperative marketing societies can be classified into two groups (i) commodity cooperative marketing societies and (ii) cooperative processing-cum-marketing societies. The cooperative societies may be dealing in production, processing or marketing depend significantly on the social structure, the group management approach and the economic environment. These factors determine the magnitude and direction of the cooperative movement leading to success or failure. The success of the primary cooperatives depend on a congenial social and economic environment for the growth and development. The experience of cooperative marketing provides considerable opportunity to build up a strong alternative channel against private lobbying. It shows group dynamics woven around common interest and resource sharing[2]. The limited opportunities for small farmers in regulated markets, bureaucratisation and political interference the market committee, traders lobbying and semi-permisibility of social structure have all brought in focus the need for community production. In due course of time it has stimulated the social dynamism for cooperativisation in many sectors to draw better monetary benefits within the existing rural economic systems.

Social Dynamics

In economical context the rural society can be classified into two categories (i) benefitted class and (ii) suppressed class. It has been a social phenomenon since the ages that the large farmers or then so called zamindars exploited the small farmers through money lending, trading and other socio-economic obligations. In such social structure, the rural power configuration rests against the interests of suppressed class, say small farmers and household entrepreneurs in rural areas. The major reason for such consequence may be the low productivity, disorganised and economically feeble conditions due to which the rural producers are unable to withstand established market forces. These circumstances originated and encouraged the cooperative organisation with specific objectives like production, processing or marketing. It has been a people's participation to a large extent as it cannot be forced through government intervention. It was not evident so even in target group community programmes. The experience of 'Pani Panchayat' (Water Council) in Maharashtra gives considerable clues and evidences of social dynamics[3].

The social needs in developing economics gave way to diversified participating and cooperative approaches. As such different commodity cooperatives, thrift societies, different agricultural activity cooperatives like, land development cooperatives, irrigation, tree growers cooperatives etc., have emerged. The cooperatives in non-farm sector exclusively for rural women has also significant development in the cooperative movement. The coir fibre cooperatives in the east-coastal belt in the country covering the States Kerala, Tamil Nadu, Andhra Pradesh and parts of the Orissa have developed in non-farm sector. In coastal districts of Andhra Pradesh namely East Godavari, West Godavari, Krishna, Srikakulam and Visakhapatnam the coir fibre activities are taken up exclusively by rural women. It has distinguished features of cooperative organisational and functional pattern. These societies are primary in nature and are efficiently performing at grass roots level with local backward and forward linkage. They exercise their autonomy, independent economy and the social status. Thus the need was felt in study such systems managed by rural women in cooperative sector as a principal activity of income generation.

The Study Region

The East Godavari district has been purposively selected for the study[4]. The fibre activities are concentrated in Godavari Central Delta region which is administratively earmarked as Amalapuram division. The East Godavari district constitute 3 administrative zones namely (i) agency area (ii) upland area and (iii) delta area. The major occupation in the region is predominantly agriculture with paddy as staple crop. The coconut plantation is the additional source of income in the region which is common for large farmers to land less labourers. It provides many activities in non-farm sector. The fibre industry is one among them[5].

The Sample

The coir fibre industry is a household activity in the region. In all there are ten fibre cooperatives organised and managed by rural women. To conduct the study 50 per cent of the societies were covered and the primary schedules were adminstered to 12 members in each society. These in all 60 member women were selected for the study. Table 4.1 exhibits the size of the society and the proportion of the sample selected for data collection.

The overall sample size consist of 38.46 per cent to the total membership of the selected societies. These societies are located in 4 mandals. The society also procure the manufactued products from non-members of the same village. However, it is observed that on an average there is one member per house in the village.

Table 4.1: Sampling Design for Fibre Cooperatives Study

Sl. No.	Name of the Society and Place	Code	Member-ship	Sample members	Percen-tage to total
1.	Narendra Coir Industrial Cooperative Society, Narendrapuram	NRP	30	12	40.0
2.	Mahalakshmi Coir Industrial Cooperative Society, Potavaram	PTR	51	12	23.52
3.	Ramachandra Fibre Industrial Cooperative Society, Perur	PRR	30	12	40.0
4.	Balaji Coir Workers Industrial Cooperative Society, Gannavaram	GNV	20	12	60.0
5.	Boduskura Coir Industrial Cooperative Society, Bodukura	BDS	25	12	48.0
	Overall		156	60	38.46

The Economy

The coir industry is the main activity in the non-farm sector and is popular at household lev^l among the landless. in the region, there are small scale industries for extracting the coir fibre from coconut husk. These are commonly two types of coir fibre found in the coastal areas, namely (i) white fibre and (ii) brown fibre. The coastal areas in Andhra Pradesh produce brown fibre to large extent. The major work is handled by women in manufacturing coir products in the study region. The cooperatativisation of this household industry began in 1978 and initially 4 cooperative societies were established. These societies were revised in 1985 to get in streamline of functioning. The foregoing discussion deal with various economic aspects of the coir fibre industrial cooperative societies in the study region.

Profile of Respondents

The women members of selected cooperatives for the study were landless and adapted the coir fibre works as a principal occupation. It was found that all the members were lying below poverty line earning less than Rs.4,800 per annum. Table 4.2 exhibits the participation per family in the village cooperatives. It can be seen from the Table that 69.06 per cent of total respondents were found having annual income between Rs.2501-4000. The average family size constitute of 5 members with membership of two person in 21.89 per cent of households. Table 4.3 shows the level of education of the members of cooperatives.

Table 4.2: Socio-economic Characteristics of Respondents

Sl. No.	*Society Code*	*Total Membership*	*Average family size of members*	*Annual Income [Rs]*	
				> 2500	*2501-4000*
1.	NRP	30	5	4 (13.33)	26 (86.67)
2.	PTR	51	4	16 (31.37)	16.35 (68.63)
3.	PRR	30	6	9 (30.0)	21 (70.0)
4.	GNV	20	5	12 (60.0)	8 (40.0)
5.	BDS	25	4	5 (20.0)	20 (80.0)
	Overall	156	4.8	46 (30.94)	110 (69.06)

Figures in parantheses indicate percentage to column 3 in each row.

The data reveals that about half of the cooperative members are illiterate. However 49.36 per cent to the total sample were found educated up to primary standards.

Growth of Cooperatives

The coir fibre industrial cooperative societies in East Godavari district have started in mid eighties and have been functioning within the village. It was found that during the period of revival of these cooperatives, all the households in the village were made members of the society. However the number is reduced in some societies and same are yet continuing with the same strength of members. The societies also entertain non-members for the purpose of procurement of coir fibre articles from them. It is observed that in due course of time the number of non-members are increased. It indicates that these societies have expanded their business in open market. The society does not supply the raw material and implements to the non-members but procures the manufactured items from them. Table 4.4 exhibits the growth in fibre cooperatives in the region.

Table 4.3: Level of Education of Cooperative Members

S.No.	*Society Code*	*Level of Education*			
		Illiterate	*Primary*	*Above Primary*	*Total*
1.	NRP	5	23	2	30
2.	PTR	20	31	-	51
3.	PRR	22	8	-	30
4.	GNV	14	6	-	20
5.	BDS	15	9	1	25
	Overall	76 (48.72)	77 (49.36)	3 (1.92)	156 (100)

Figures in parantheses indicate percentage to row total.
Source: Survey Method.

Table 4.4: Growth in Membership of Fibre Cooperatives

Sl. No.	*Society Code*	*1985*	*1987*	*1991*	*CGR (%) Base 1987*
1.	NRP	-	27	30	2.67
2.	PTR	-	35	51	9.87
3.	PRR	92	107	127*	4.38
4.	GNV	74	74	74*	0.0
5.	BDS	58	58	55*	(-)1.32

CGR : Compound Growth Rate in per cent w.r.t. base year 1987.
* includes non-working members.
Source: Survey Method and Society Documents.

The data reveals that the growth in membership is not high. It may be due to the limited operational status of the societies.

Forward Linkages

The organisational strength to the primary societies have been provided by setting up forward linkages through government intervention. However due to lack of proper administrative set-up and functional demarcation the organisational linkages are not effective. The Diagram 4.1 illustrates the forward linkages set up for the primary coir fibre industrial cooperatives in the East Godavari district.

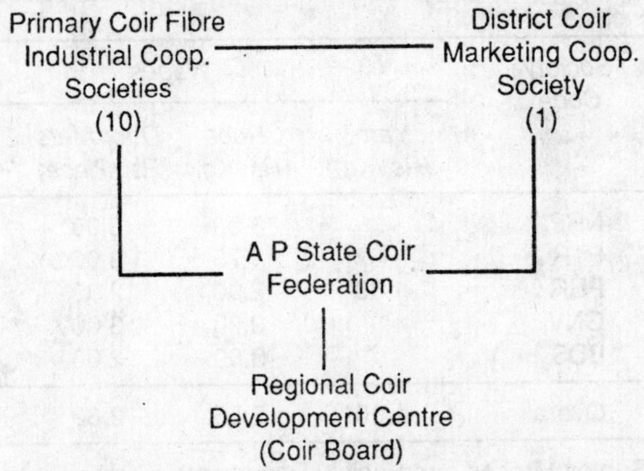

Diagram 4.1: Organisational Linkage to Primary Fibre Coops.

Regional Coir Development Centre (RCDC) of Coir Board imports skills and training to the members of primary co-operatives. The District Coir Marketing Cooperative Society is set up at Rajmundry a commercial town in the district to channelise the products manufactured by the primary societies in open market. The Coir Federation has to prompt the coir industrial cooperatives in the state and to provide support in production, technology and marketing. However these institutions could not come through successfully in establishing their objectives. The primary cooperatives have local backward and forward linkages. The RCDC is imparting technical know how to the managers of the primary cooperatives. The Coir Board has also adopted Perur (Society Code PRR) for overall development and the RCDC is monitoring the socio-economic level change in the village. It can be stated that the primary cooperatives are dynamic in marketing management with their own resources. The District Rural Development Agency (DRDA) has provided the infrastructure i.e., workshop and implements to the society of worth Rs.1 lakh each.

Production

The production system in the societies is wage oriented. The wages are subject to the articles manufactured by the members per day. The members of the societies commonly manufacture reap and door mats.

Table 4.5: Wage Pattern in Fibre Cooperatives

S. No	*Society Code*	*Wages*			
		Yarn (Rs./Kg.)	*Rope (Rs./Kg.)*	*Door Mats (Rs./Piece)*	*Carpet (Rs./Mtr.)*
1.	NRP	-	3.00	3.00	-
2.	PTR	-	1.75	3.00	4.00
3.	PRR	1.00	2.00	2.00	4.00
4.	GNV	-	3.00	3.00	-
5.	BDS	-	3.00	2.00	-
	Overall	1.00	2.55	2.60	4.00

Source: Survey Method and Society Documents.

However some skilled members manufacture coir fibre carpets on looms. The wages paid for different products in the societies is exhibited in Table 4.5.

It can be seen from the data that there is no uniformal wage pattern is followed in the societies. It was found that the wages are determined according to average rate of production and turnover per day. Since there is no State support on marketing of products, the Federation is unable to formulate a uniformal wage structure and impose regulation.

It is observed that a member can either manufacture rope or door mats or weave carpet in a day. Thus by limitative of time and physical strength, a member concentrates on either of these works and earns subsistance income. The activities of coir fibre are largely carried by group of members except the manufacture of door mats. The quantity of articles manufactured by group members are divided and wages are paid accordingly. Table 4.6 depicts the production and income of members engaged in manufacturing of different products. The data reveals that on an average a member earns Rs.236.5 per month. The wages for carpet weaving are general an additional income to the skilled workers. The raw material i.e. the fibre is procured from local plants. It is found that on an average 1.55 tonnes of coir fibre is used in the societies. They do incur transportation charges at the rate of Rs.1 per bale of 50 Kgs. Thus in a month the expenditure towards transportation will be Rs.339 on an average. Table 4.7 exhibits the consumption of raw material in different societies.

Table 4.6: Production and Income of Members
(Rupees per month per member)

Sl. No.	*Society Code*	*Quantity Manufactured*				*Income Realised*			
		P1 (Kg.)	*P2 (Kg.)*	*P3 (No.)*	*P4 (Mtr.)*	*P1*	*P2*	*P3*	*P4*
1.	NRP	-	60	9	-	-	180	270	-
2.	PTR	-	90	60	30	-	157.5	180	120
3.	PRR	240	150	150	40	240	300	300	160
4.	GNV	-	90	90	-	-	270	270	-
5.	BDS	-	60	120	-	-	180	240	-
	Overall	240	90	102	35	240	217.5	252	140

P1 : Yarn P2 : Rope P3 : Door Mats P4 : Carpet
Source: Survey Method.

Table 4.7: Consumption and Cost of Raw Material

S. No.	*Society Code*	*Consumption of Raw Material (Tonne/Month)*	*Value of Raw Material (Rs./Month)*
1.	NRP	1.5	2,400
2.	PTR	1.5	2,400
3.	PRR	2.0	3,200
4.	GNV	1.25	2,000
5.	BDS	1.5	2,400
	Overall	1.55	2,480

Source: Survey Method.

The products manufactured by the members of the society are not graded. They have largely local market. The products are commonly graded in the open market as coarse and medium and retailed accordingly. The members are not properly skilled in mat and carpet weaving, though the RCDC and District Industries Centre are making efforts to render proper extension services. By and large it is found that the lack of contact persons to impart technical knowledge at society level has bagged down the skill development opportunities. There is one Technical Assistant to attend on the technological development of all the cooperatives in the district, which is highly improportionate.

Marketing

It is found during the study that there is a localised market for the coir fibre products manufactured by the societies. The petty traders visit the societies fornightly and procure the products who channelise through wholesalers and to bulk consumers and retailers. The Diagram 4.2 exhibits the existing marketing channels for fibre products in the region.

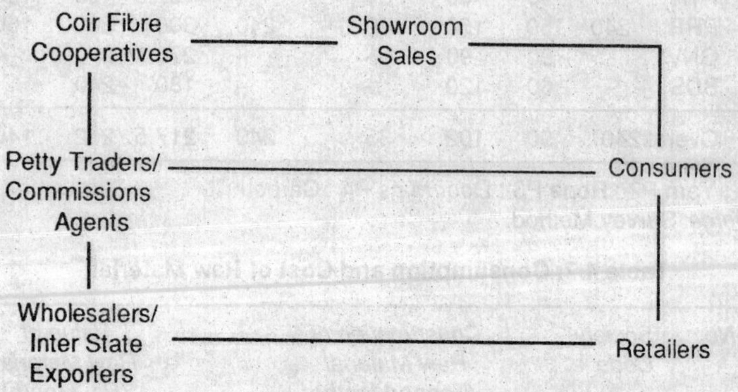

Diagram 4.2: Marketing Channels in the Rural Fibre Industry

On some occasions the wholesalers also procure from the societies and also place contract orders. The fibre products are exported to Maharashtra, Madhya Pradesh and Uttar Pradesh from this region and the wholesalers many times act as exporters for these States. The Petty Traders in all practical sense act as Commission Agents of wholesalers. They are given advance money for procurement and on the total value of purchases 3 per cent commission is paid.

The societies sell the produce at relatively higher prices and earn profit which is distributed as dividend annually among the members. The private traders are the only channel available to the society. There is no transport cost involved in the part of the society. There are weekly markets held around the societies but due to uncertainity of sales, the preference is given to private traders. Table 4.8 exhibits the structure of sales price coopted by the traders and society. It can be seen from the table that the doormats and ropes are high price fetching. In context to Table 4.5 it can be stated that the society sells the products like rope and door mats at 2.47 and 2.65 time more than the wages paid for the same quantity.

Table 4.8: Price Structure for Sales of Products

Sl. No.	Society Code	Products			
		Yarn (Rs./Kg.)	Rope (Rs./Kg.)	Doormats (Rs./Unit)	Carpet (Rs./Mtr)
1.	NRP	-	6.0	6.0	-
2.	PTR	-	5.5	5.0	35.00
3.	PRR	6.0	7.0	8.0	34.00
4.	GNV	-	6.5	7.0	-
5.	BDS	-	6.5	8.5	-
	Overall	6.0	6.3	6.9	34.5

Source: Society Documents.

It is found that wholesalers and retailers earn 15 and 22 per cent margin over the products purchased from the societies. Table 4.9 analyses the producer's share in the consumers rupee on various products manufactured by the society. The data reveals that the producers share is higher in rope manufacturing as compared to other two types of product. Since the door mats and carpets have lesser demand in market as compared to the rope, the margin of profit taken by intermediate channels are more. Such incidence reduces the producers' share finally in consumers' rupee. The table reveals that 72.25 per cent share goes to producers from the final price in rope marketing while only 54.33 per cent is realised in door mats. The products other than rope are used in small quantity and are not dispensable in short span. Thus it is found that the market demand for such products move slowly and so higher margin on marketing is realised by the intermediate channels.

Table 4.9: Producers' Share in Consumers' Rupee

Sl. No.	*Particulars/ Products*	*Rope (Rs. Kg.)*	*Doormats (Rs./Unit)*	*Carpet (Rs./Mtr.)*
1.	Society's selling price (Pp)	6.3	6.9	34.5
2.	Wholesalers' price (Pw)	8.5	8.0	46.0
3.	Retailers' price (Pr)	12.0	13.5	60.0
4.	Weighted average price (Pwrp)	8.72	12.70	53.68
5.	Producers share (per cent) [(P = Pwrp)x100]	72.25	54.33	64.27

Source : Computed based on Survey data.

The producers' share in consumers rupee is computed using the formula as below:

$$Pwrp = \frac{Pw.Mn + Pr.Mr}{Mn + Mr} \quad \ldots (i)$$

$$Pc = [Pp\ Pwrp] \times 100 \quad \ldots (ii)$$

Where in equation (i),

Pwrp Weighted average price of products
Pw Wholesaler's price
Pr Retailer's price
Mn Wholesaler's price
Mr Retailer's margin

Whereas in equation (ii)

Pc Producer's share in consumer's rupee
Pp Producer's price (society's selling price)

It can be stated that the manufacturing and marketing of rope is more profitable as compared to other products undertaken by the societies as far as open market is concerned. The data on production and sales of different items is exhibited in Table 4.10 which reveals that the sales realisation is more than 85 per cent of the production value. It indicates that the demand and product mobility in the open market is high and uninterrupted to large extent.

Table 4.10: Business Status of Fibre Cooperatives (90-91)

(Amount in Rupees)

Sl. No.	*Society Code*	*Production*	*Sales*
1.	NRP	26,120.0	22,725.0 (87.00)
2.	PTR	7,587.0	9,328.0 (122.94)
3.	PRR	35,913.0	30,627.0 (85.28)

Source: Official Document
Figures in parantheses is percentage to Column 3.

The economy of the primary cooperatives discussed in this chapter show that these societies are developed on local resource roots. They are largely dependent on the local traders. It is found that the society's wage structure and earning widely vary as the members are low paid compared to the sales realisation. The technical input in the society is also poor which reflect in the production of contemporary designs and quality, products. However the societies are functioning with objectives of providing local employment to landless women workers and subsistence income.

The Future

The coir fibre industrial cooperatives in the study region are functioning at subsistence economic levels as a local source of employment and income generation. Since it is a need based organisation it is functioning largely on mutual trust and loyalty rather than any set principles on cooperative line. By and large it may be defined as a thrift group of rural women. However, the coir cooperatives with exclusive participation of rural women in the region have shown better results than the societies organised at larger scale such as handloom, bamboo and cane workers and cobblers' cooperatives in rural industrial sector. These coir fibre societies are functioning since 1985 after revival by the industries department of the state, but could not achieve significant economic growth. The study revealed that the basic reason for such economic condition is the lack of proper state patronage at the enbryonic stage of the societies especially in the field of production and marketing. The prospects of these societies are subject to the establishment of effective backward and forward linkages. The existing status of the societies show that they do not have appropriate linkages. The foregoing text discusses the problems and future prospects of fibre cooperatives for rural women.

Organisational Structure

The societies have an integrated organisational structure of members, government nominees, and coopted members. Since these societies are at the grass roots level, the management decision taken by the society largely depend on the government departments for the implementation with DRDA and DIC. The Technical Assistant of the societies who also act as a liason officer for the government has a wide jurisdiction which do not permit him to act efficiently all the time. The local political environment has substantial control over the organisational and Management decision. The Diagram 4.3 exhibits the organisational pattern and the configuration of local power structure.

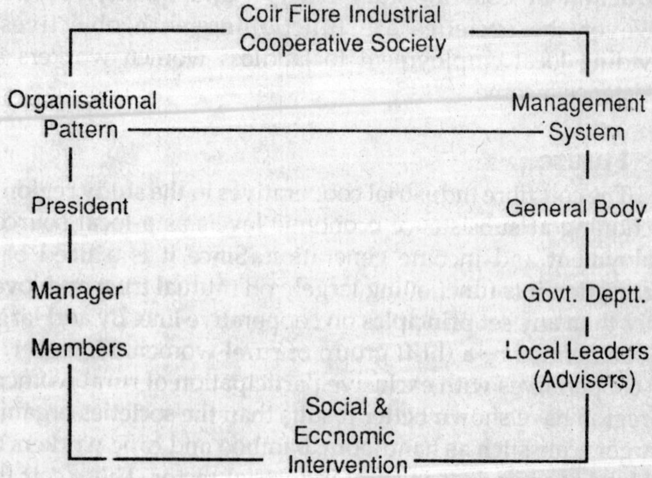

Diagram 4.3: Organisational Configuration of the Society

The president and general body members are elected among the all member workers. It was found during the study that in all 47.81 per cent of the coir workers have economic obligation of the rural rich who are also active in local politics. Such conditions pave path for open interframe in the activities of rural cooperatives which some times lead to distress and affect the autonomy. The Technical Assistant is one of the nominees in the society while another post is vacant in all the selected societies. The Managers of the societies are paid and answerable to the general body. The danger foreseen in these cooperatives during the study is the intervention of local traders who have also political patronage may indirect economical ailments in the society leading internal parching of organisation.

Skills and Technology

The selected societies have conventional production technology. The production of ropes, door mats and furnishing are manually done which reduces the quality and affects the demand. The members have the traditional skills acquainted from the elder generations. The skills to produce new designs of furnishing, quality rope is not developed among the members. Table 4.11 shows the status of training acquired by the members on rope making and furnishing designing.

Table 4.11: Training on Fibre Products Manufacturing (1990-91)

Sl. No.	*Society Code*	*Field of Training*	*Duration/ Organisation*	*No. of Members*
1.	NRP	Weaving	6 months (TRY)	10
2.	PTR	Weaving	6 months (TRY)	22
3.	PRR	Mating	4 weeks (RCDC)	5
4.	GNV	Weaving	6 months (TRY)	15
5.	BDS	Mating	4 weeks (RCDC)	8
	Overall			60

Figures in parantheses indicate percentage to total membership of selected societies. TRY : TRYSEM RCDC : Regional Coir Development Centre.
Source: Survey Method.

The TRYSEM training is given locally without any input on the advanced production and designing aspects. Since the society has to bear the cost of training members at RCDC it is often not possible due to paucity of funds. The lack of openings for advanced training has made the societies traditional. There is a potential market demand for the coir fibre mats and furnishing but due to lack of skills these articles are being produced with non-mechanised looms. It can be seen from the Table that 38. 46 per cent members are trained. The DIC provides the mechines at 50 per cent subsidy to the societies but they are unable to install for mainly two reasons (i) lack of trained workers to operate and (ii) under utilisation of machines.

It is observed that the factors related to skills, technology, production and marketing are interreated. The rural entrepreneurial cooperatives (RECs) like coir fibre, bamboo and cane, handloom etc., have been suffering from severe marketing set back due to lack of adoption of Advanced Techniques (ATs) related to marketing.

The traditions of rural economy and sociological aspects are so intimately related to each other, it is often difficult to distinguish the perceptional and logistic dimensions of REFs towards innovative approaches. This happens in production and marketing technologies. The components at diffusion process in marketing technology of RECs has various variables related to the social, economic and behavioural factors. The diffusion process in general, has been defined acceptance of the innovative approaches over a period of time for specific cause. It may be adopted by individuals or group under a a social structure within the given system of values or culture. However in the process of diffusion and adaption of technologies a specific communicative channel is used. Table 4.12 explains the characteristics of diffusion components in context of different variables related to social, economic behavioural and political segments. The political interference in RECs will not be much if the operational area of the marketing is not coinciding with the established town or regulated market. However the socio-economic aspects have major impact on decision making to adapt the technology/ marketing in RECs[6]. The 'time' and 'awareness' have the key elements to be considered in regard to sociological characteristics of the diffusion components. The lower the risk in adoption of innovative technology the greater will be the rate of adoption by RECs in villages. Over and above the economic advantages over the existing practices has also an important consideration in this context. All these characteristics form the base of technology diffusion and adoption.

Table 4.12: Components of Diffusion and their Characteristics

Sociological	*Economic*	*Behavioural*	*Political*
* Adoption	* Comparative advantages	* Accessibility	* Attitude of Rural Political elites
* Time	* Demand Oriented	* Interest	* External influences
* Community Benefits	* Alternative Marketing Techniques	* Scope for trial error	* Vested interest
* Awareness	* Infrastructural Support	* Close to traditional technology	* Political Lobbying
* Consensus	* Risk Management	* Within the Purview of value systems	* Level of conflicts and Management

State Intervention

The fibre cooperatives get the assistance from DRDA and DIC. The infrastructure like workshed, godown and implements to the members is being provided by the DRDAs, whereas DIC provides the machinery up to Rs.20 lakhs with subsidy of 15 to 50 per cent. The mating looms have been provided by DIC and monitors the operation through technical assistant. Table 4.13 exhibits the type of government intervention in different fields of production and allied activities. The DRDA provides maximum Rs.1 lakh at one instance for construction of workshop and godown per cooperative society. As stated in the pretext the Coir Board has adopted the Perur village and has given the society Rs.3 lakhs for building the community infrastructure during the year 1991-92. However the study found that the technical input is lacking largely in the societies and for its promotion institutional efforts to be planned with need based bottom-up approach.

Table 4.13: Government Intervention in Primary Cooperatives

Sl. No.	Agency	Type of Intervention
1.	DRDA	Infrastructure, Training Hand Operated Machines, Organising Cooperatives, Subsidy, Monitoring and Evaluation
2.	DIC	Technical assistance, training machinery, susbidy, functional subsidy (power etc.)
3.	RCDC	Training on Production and Designing
4.	Coir Board	Welfare activity, adoption of village, financing for social infrastructure

Source: Survey Method

Marketing

The crux of the whole production oriented rural economy is lack of marketing avenues for the products manufactured traditionally. The rural products are not risk resistant and so the rate of drop out is higher in cooperative market environment. The consumer demand for rural products is low as compared to the products having machine finish. The coir products produced with traditional skills also undergo such business tension and largely stand at the subsistance level either at break even point or slightly lesser than it. Table 4.14 exhibits the comparative status of demand for the coir products with machine and hand finish touch among consumers. The table reveals that there is more demand for machine finished coir products than hand finished. The institutions like schools, government offices, banks, public sector undertakings (Godavari Fertilisers)* and private sector units (Nagarjuna Fertilisers)* prefer largely machine made products as office furnishings. The rural coir products are not fetching significant price and substantial demand. Thus it is essential to improve the quality of the products of rural coir cooperatives and to achieve this the extension services with regard to training and awareness need to be enhanced.

Problems of Primary Cooperatives

It is observed during the study that the coir fibre cooperative societies in the region have the problems related to

* Units covered under survey.

technology adoption, adequate finance and training[7]. The marketing channels are however established and adequate to mobilise the stock of the societies. Table 4.15 exhibits the nature and magnitude of problems faced by the Fibre Cooperatives in the study region. The price structure is however lower as compared to the open market due to lack of proper quality. The members revealed that the wage rates paid by the societies to them for different products are low and need to be increased. Table 4.15 shows the nature of problems faced by the members of the society. The data on an average 64.58 per cent members stated the problems of getting low wage rate while 73.09 per cent expressed the problems of lack of training for production and quality improvement. The lack of individual credit facilities to the members by the society is also emerged as one of the important problems faced by the members as expressed by 55.62 per cent sample respondents. It was found that absence of electrification in the societies (40 per cent), sanitation facilities in all the societies and lack of extra common place for work are major problems faced by the members. As such 61.81 per cent members stated that the lack of infrastructure is one of major problems.

Table 4.14: Quality Differentiation in Coir Products

Sl. No.	*Consumer Segment*	*Preference for Products*	
		Machine made	*Hand finish*
1.	Urban (12)	66.67	33.33
2.	Semi-urban (12)	58.33	41.67
3.	Rural (7)	57.15	42.85
4.	Institutions (6)	83.33	16.67
	Overall (37)	53.09	46.91

Figures in parantheses indicate sample size.
Source: Survey Method.

Emerging Issues

The discussions on the concept, economy and the future of coir fibre industrial cooperatives highlights some issues for consideration about rural industrial cooperatives. The existence of such institutions depend largely on the effective coordination

Table 4.15: Problems of Coir Fibre Cooperatives
(Response in per cent)

Sl. No.	Nature of Problem	Society Code					Average
		NRP	PTR	DRR	GNV	BDS	
1.	Low Wage Rate	73.33	82.35	26.66	—	76.0	64.58
2.	Lack of Infrastructure	46.66	70.59	70.0	—	60.0	61.81
3.	Lack of individual credit	63.33	56.86	46.66	—	—	55.62
4.	Lack of Training in Mating	86.66	76.47	53.33	65.0	84.0	73.09
5.	Lack of Graded Prices	36.66	41.78	—	80.0	—	52.61

Source: Survey Method.

of various socio-economic factors. Of these, there emerges some issues of organisational and functional importance. They are as under:

(i) Whether the existing pattern of leadership in rural industrial cooperatives where the subsistence level entrepreneurs work together, is in right direction? What motivational and behavioural approaches need to be considered in rural areas.

(ii) The status of production economy in coir cooperatives reveal that they lack in technology adoption, finance and contemporary skills. Under these conditions what should be the role of state intervention in uplifting. The rural economy of artisans through organised efforts. There is a need to draw a policy of the government towards upgrading the skills and providing applicable technology at par to their socio-economic conditions.

(iii) The study reveals that rural industrial cooperatives on coir fibre do not have proper accounting system as they are not regularly audited by the Govenment. The societies maintain the daily cash accounts but they have not attempted to keep the annual acounts and audited balance sheet. The Managers, though had undergone cash training on corporative accounts but literally lack in proper guidance. In absence of proper accounts, it is difficult to monitor and evaluate any cooperative society. The issue in context to above lacunae emerges is to handover the supervision and analysis of accounting and auditing system to NGOs as a people group to monitor the societies and develop necessary social checks.

(iv) The promotion of institutional marketing for bulk purchasing of the coir products as furnishing items need to be developed. The issue of involvement of DRDA and DSMS need to considered as a policy perspective to promote the marketing institutionally. It would be a better option to develop as an alternative channel and

(v) The cooperative extension work need a dynamic start in rural areas. The NGOs may be entertained in such field where a social and personal approach is required instead of an administrative look out on the development of rural cooperatives.

These issues need substantial discussion and consideration from an applied and perspective angle.

References

1. Reserve Bank of India : All India Rural Credit Survey: Report of the Committee on Direction (Vol. II), The General Report, Bombay, 1954.
2. Rajagopal: Dynamics of Cooperative Marketing in India : Its Magnitude and Direction, Working Paper, NIRD, 1991.
3. Deshpande RS and Ratna Reddy : Social Dynamics & Farmers' Society, A case study of Pani Panchayat, Indian Journal of Agricultural Economics, 45 (3), July-Sept. 1990, pp. 355-61.
4. Government of Andhra Pradesh : Performance of DRDA, Internal Report, DRDA, East Godavari Dist., Kakinada, 1990.
5. Rajagopal : Indian Agriculture : An Analysis of Backward and Forward linkages, Inter-India Publications, New Delhi, 1990, pp. 94-110.
6. Rajagopal : Difrusion and Adoption : Marketing Technologies in Rural Areas, Workshop Paper, Workshop on Marketing Support for Rural Development Programmes, NIRD, Sept. 9-10, 1991.
7. Rajagopal : Linkages in IRDP : Lessons from States, Kurukshetra, April, 1991.

5

Marketing Technology

The dynamism of marketing environment is reflected in demand shifts, product designs, market promotion strategies and consumer communication. The frequent changes in marketing practices involve high risk in terms of the sales realisation and the consumer acceptance in the long term. The marketing innovations which are the change agents constitute reformation of the traditional or existing methods or introduction of the new approaches altogether for marketing of products and services in the intra and inter regional markets. By and large, such innovation is a complex process, which requires the use of knowledge in order to generate common interest in adoption of an innovative technology. The rural entrepreneurs being less exposed to the marketing ethic, possess more reluctance towards change in the prevailing practices and thus, show less significant impact on the overall outcome of the diffused innovation as compared to the urban areas.

Cyclical Behaviour

The process of innovation in a society passes through various stages and seldom take place at a given spatial framework. However it is participated by the different persons and organisations. The model of product market innovation process in a social context is illustrated in Diagram 5.1. The long-run acceptance of such change in rural areas lead to adoption of the change. However to achieve this objective it is essential to have homogeneous diffussion of advance technologies [ATs] of marketing in rural areas to create awareness about the comparative advantages of the change.

In rural entrepreneurial firms [REFs], engaged in farm or non-farm activities function with various pre-conceptions on social and economic factors which prevent them from developing a cohesive environment for adopting the change order. Such behaviour develops non-development barriers and do not allow to cross the traditional system of production and marketing. The process of innovation in marketing takes a long time but there are considerable differences between inter and intra regional approaches due to heterogeneous and homogeneous conditions respectively. Some of the major innovations in farm sector are the mechanisation of cultivation practices particularly in the dry land conditions towards the field operations and improved cultivation practices like use of HYV packages including fertilisers and

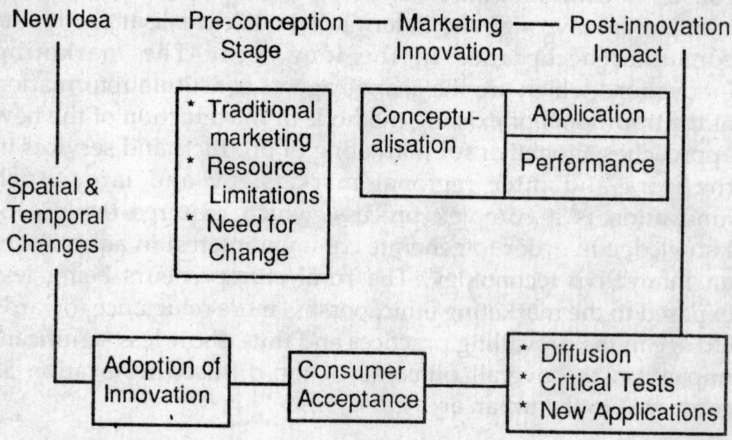

Diagram 5.1: Diffusion and Adoption in Innovative Marketing

pesticides for the dry land crops, soil conservation and watershed management and the post-harvest technology. On the other side of non-farm sector innovations that took place in the recent past are notably in the production and marketing of processed food items, garments, handlooms, paper pulp and allied products. The innovations in the technological front in the farm and non-farm sector took 6-24 years for the first realisation at the break-even in the society[1]. The diffusion of ATs in rural areas face a greater constraint of acceptability as they are largely communicated without appropriate empirical support. Thus the commonly identified gap between the diffusion of ATs and adoption is the applied concepts with emphasis on the felt needs of the user groups which helps in gaining the social confidence. Of late, the user acceptance to the adoption of ATs adds strength to the

Diagram 5.2 Theoritical Diffusion and Adoption Curve of ATs of Marketing in Varying Spatial and Temporal Dynamics

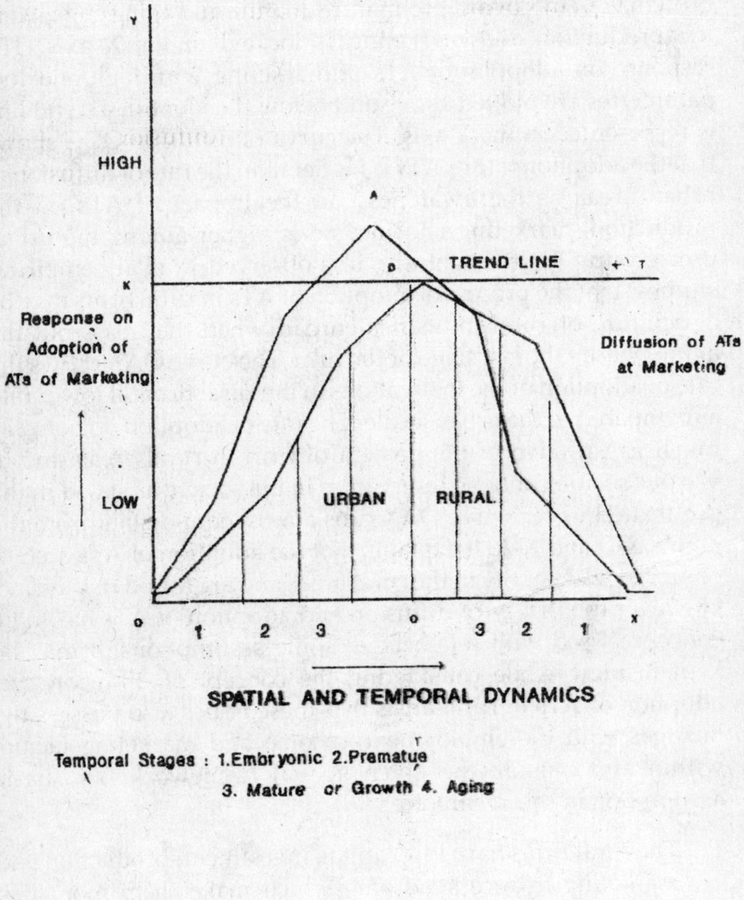

Temporal Stages : 1.Embryonic 2.Prematue 3. Mature or Growth 4. Aging

behavioural dimensions towards an established change[2]. Howeve- the spatial and temporal effects over the period of time may put the process into the cyclical system for the next generation of user group.

The theoretical interpretation to the process of diffusion is exhibited in the Diagram 5.2 under specific assumptions. The spatial and temporal aspects of a firm possessing four stages of growth viz. embroynic, pre-mature, mature and aging engaged in the production and marketing is located in the X axis. The response on adoption of ATs of marketing with high and low parametres are plotted above and below the identified trend line is represented in the Y axis. The curve of diffusion ODC shows that the adoption rate of ATs is higher than the rate of diffusion in urban areas as the awareness on the impact of ATs on the production, marketing and income is higher among the urban user groups. On the contrary, it is observed in many empirical studies[3] that the process of adoption of ATs in rural firms may be agriculture or rural industries enroad when they pass out the aging phase - the last stage of the firm. The curve OAX shows the rate of adoption of the innovations in the rural firms at lower rate as compared to the urban locale. The rate of adoption do not vary much irrespective of the growth of firm in rural areas due to various socio-economic reservation in the society as stated in the pre-text. Thus the curve OAX runs almost equi-distant from the points X-D and X-A. It explains that the adoption of ATs are not observed unilaterally in the rural areas and are found risk averse. However the theory of diffusion and adoption of ATs has to be conceptualised with reference to some assumptions. It may be kept in view while considering the concept of diffusion and adoption of ATs in rural areas that these issues also possess the linkages with the employment, income and marketing factors within and outside the given spatial framework. The basic assumption in this regard are :

1. The rural firms have low capital, investment, production and marketing finance syndrome which make ihem more risk averse as compared to the capital oriented firms in urban areas.
2. The market for the products resulting the adoption of ATs is not assured and the risk prevails in the open market.

3. The use of ATs are capital oriented and need extension education.
4. The rural firms largely prefer to minimise the risk than maximising the profit.

'KAP' Analysis

The behavioural dimensions influence the decision making on various functional issues in rural firms to a large extent. The aspects related to knowledge, attitude, and practice [KAP] constitute the core behavioural determinents which have major role in the adoption process of ATs. The Table 5.1 exhibits the major knowledge types required for diffusion and adoption of ATs in rural firms to improve the overall status. It can be seen from the Table that knowledge on all the indicators exists with the organised entrepreneurs and they possess the ability to use them. However, there is a need for comprehensive diffusion of ATs horizontally and vertically in the rural society. Although the operational knowledge is available with the unorganised sector entrepreneurs, the awareness about the product, market demand and price is almost absent. The knowledge about the production process is conventional in UREs and needs induction of an intermediated technology appropriate to the socio-economic conditions thereof. Since the UREs largely function at the subsistance level of economy the scientific knowledge of production and marketing mix and their application is also essential after the attitude building towards the adoption of ATs in farm and non-farm sectors.

The institutional support is therefore, a pre-requisite for the adoption of the ATs pertaining to any innovation in the farm and non-farm sectors production and marketing to insure against the risk and uncertainty. The production and process know-how not only refers to technical and managerial skills required for adoption but also need the understanding on the production and business logistics. The penetration of the knowledge on the above issues will synthesise the KAP behaviour and its magnitude in the society in the vertical or horizontal direction.

In regard to marketing the spatial movement of the products from high to low demand concentration areas may be defined as vertical expansion e. g. Urban——Semi-urban——Rural. The diffusion of production technology also follows the same path in VE while the intra regional diffusion in rural areas e.g. Village 1——Village 2——Village 3, may be defined as horizontal expansion in the diffusion of production and marketing technology.

Table 5.1: Requirement of Knowledge in Adoption Process

	Knowledge Type	*Availability*	*Status*		*Requirement*
			OE	*URE*	
1.	Production and process know-how	OE/URE	AT	CN	IT
2.	Market demand for product	OE	AT	—	CE
3.	Knowledge of product and marketing mix	OE/URE	AT	SM	IS
4.	Innovation management	OE/URE	RA	—	PMA
5.	Business expansion	OE/URE	VE	HE	VE

OE = Organised entrepreneurs, URE = Unorganised rural entrepreneurs, AT = Advance technology, CE = Common exposure, CN = Conventional, IT = Intermediate technology, SM = Subsistance marketing, IS = Institutional support, RA = Risk averse, PMA = Production and market assurance, VE = Vertical expansion, HE = Horizontal expansion.

The available knowledge, requirements and the gap therein develop further components 'attitude' and 'practice' towards adoption of diffused technology. The development of attitude is a process which includes many goal oriented perceptions on the production and marketing technology over a period of time. The motivational factors in developing the attitude and practice to lead a phenomenal change may be termed a 'drive' stands significantly in this context. The Diagram 5.3 exhibits the association between the attitude and practice in technology extension. It is a process and faces many social and economic interventions[4]. The traditional and cultural patterns, lack of economic efficiency, lack of achievement motivation, external locus of market control and a sub-culture of poverty have over ridden the development concerns to accept the change in practice in rural areas. Thus a larger number of UREs in farm and non-farm sectors are associated with the resistance to change in a given time.

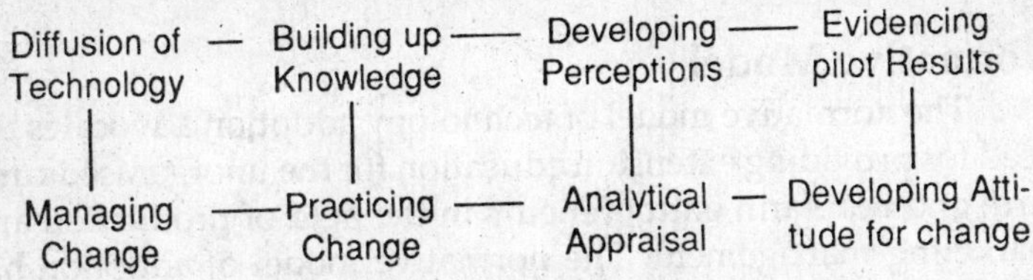

Diagram 5.3: Syncronised Attitude and Practice in Change Management

Targetting Diffusion

The diffusion research empirically demonstrated that the new technology and innovations once introduced into a social system, spread there from one decision making unit to another either individuals, household or groups to the next unit over time. It is therefore essential to identify the target segment to streamline the effectiveness of the diffused technology. Thus the 'target category' is called for observing the positive change with the spatial and temporal limitations[5]. Broadly such categorisation may be termed as 'progressive entrepreneur approach' [PEA]. There are various social, economic and behavioural factors to be considered essentially in context to the PEA. The Table 5.2 exhibits the principal factors and issues associated with the adoption attitude of PEA. The issues dealt in the Table also confirm the theory of commercial marketing[6].

Table 5.2: Factors Associated with the PEA in Technology Adoption

	Broad Areas	*Associated Issues*
1.	Demographic categories	* Heterogeneous population * Inter-class variations are high * Intra-class variations are low.
2.	Decision Making	* Socio-economic intervention in system * Inter- and Intra- class behavioural dimensions
3.	Information Base	* Technology penetration in production and marketing system * Effective dissemination of information for decision making

Normative Model

The normative model of technology adoption advocates the need for providing extension education for the unorganised rural farm and non-farm entrepreneurs in the field of production and marketing management. The normative model of adoption has five major inter-linked sub-systems viz. need for extension education [1], research [2], policy making [3], technology dessemination [4] and application by the user groups [5]. The sub-system [1] deals with the identification of knowledge, need, social and economic requirement at producers' level and attempts to induce innovations in the system. However dissemination of information for operationalising the applied concepts are also very significant issues in the sub-system [1]. The sub-system [2] and [3] are closely associated with each other. The need based research helps in evolving appropriate policies for the diffusion and motivation for adopting ATs by the rural farm and non-farm entrepreneurs. The development of technology for the common interest of the target group for introducing higher productivity and cost effectiveness is explained in the sub-system [4]. The sub-system [5] is packed with the behavioural dimensions of the group response on the technology diffused for adoption.

The INTERPAK model[7] on diffusion and adoption of technology in agriculture has skipped the considerations of socio-economic factors which are the barriers in true sense in decision making in developing countries. Thus, it is essential to promote the technology extension through peoples' participatory approaches in order to regard the felt need of the people and the socio-economic barriers in adoption of technology.

Post Adoptation Strategies

The adoption of ATs in product marketing, particularly the concept of packaging and branding is consumer oriented and need to be evaluated periodically to understand the market environment. The adoption of ATs of marketing need to be analysed from the point of view of establishing the product portfolio, strategy building for profit maximisation, cost-benefit approximation and creating demand influence. The strategy building for profit making has to pass through many uncontrollable environmental and market features. The overall market growth, inflation the extent of import-export competition and market communication are usually determined by the external forces rather than the management choice. Thus a firm venturing into the competititve market environment with ATs of marketing should also analyse the environmental effect generated outside the system[8].

Besides the market environment, the structural factors also attribute to the strategy building for product marketing in the post adoption of ATs of marketing. The competitive strategy in all practical sense entails adoption of ATs to the structural realities of the market. Thus, the competitive strategy of a firm should include :

1. The bargaining power of the consumers and suppliers;
2. The threat of new entrants with similar marketing technologies;
3. The threat of substitute products or services and
4. Rivalary among the existing firms.

The secondary objective of adopting ATs of marketing should be to generate stimulation marketing which refers to creating positive demand for a product which is absent or dorment since long span. This process involves altering the environment to increase the real value of the product e.g. a TV manufacturing company may try to stimulate the consumer demand by switching a positive brand of own, hired or collaboratively agreed, adopting ATs of marketing by supplementing the product with warranty of additional services. It is implied that the company should also do some changes in quality of the product when the ATs are conceived.

The adoption of ATs of marketing should redefine the product by changing the market environment. This speciality of a firm will allow the product to enter into the market that did not exist with a product that did not exist. Therefore the ATs should be subject to a new market expedition altogether.

Reflecting Pricing Decisions

The adoption of ATs of marketing pertaining to advertisement, packaging and branding resolve to high capital liabilities so it becomes essential for a firm to strike a balance on investments and profit. In such situation pricing decisions play crucial role in salvaging the firm out of deficit economy. In this process it is required to determine the preference of the customer, the competitors' performance, consumer needs and market segmentation. Such analysis will help in positioning the product and pace the market environment to project the profitable price package. On arriving at a successful product position, a firm should determine the following issues to introduce a price package :

1. The short list of major brands and packaging systems existing in the market.
2. Marginal costs of competing brands;
3. Value of trade-off measures;
4. Volume of purchase and
5. Customers' short list of brands.

Such analysis may not give a guarantee for optimal pricing strategy. However, subjective considerations are always needed. It is crucial to look as many facets of price as possible with regard to determinants listed above to secure a secure a consistent and a well founded strategy.

References

1. Swaminathan M S : Agricultural in 2000 AD in India, Presidential speech in IV National Seminar on Agricultural Marketing of ISAM, Pune June 3-5. 1990.
2. Rajagopal : Fruits and Vegetables Marketing in Cooperative Sector, IRMA Case Study., Anand, India, 1991.
3. Rajagopal : Input Supply and Marketing Assistance to IRDP Beneficiaries : A Study in Goa State, NIRD Research Report, Hyderabad, India, 1992.
4. Roling Niels : Extension Science : Information System for Agricultural Development, Cambridge, Cambridge Univ. Press, 1988.
5. Sabatien P & Mazamanian D : Implementation of Public Policy : A Framework of Analysis, Policy Studies Journal, 8[2], pp 583-60, (1980).
6. Kotler Phillip : Marketing for Non-Profit Organisations, Englewood Cliffs, NJ Prentice-Hall Inc., (1975).
7. Swanson B : Agricultural Knowledge System : The INTERPAKS Experience, Wageningen, IAC Plannery Session Paper [Private Circulation], 1985.
8. Varadrajan P R et. al. : Controlling the Uncontrollable : Managing Your Market Environment, Sloan Management Review, 33[2], Winter, pp. 39-48, (1992).

6

Risk and Threats in Rural Marketing

A few words like 'hazard', 'danger', 'chance' etc. provide little help in defining the linguistic meaning of the term 'RISK' as delineated in the dictionaries. Such definitions are too simple to explain the complexities of the matter of risk in product marketing where the degree of product-market environment and the personal confidence of the marketeer is equally important. Risk can be interpreted as uncertainity in the given situation in which one manager would regard high risk as a state of blockade to growth while the same may be regarded by another as worth to try. However, it may be stated that risk is a perception alike beauty that lies in the eye of the beholder.

An entrepreneur in rural areas who plays dual role of a producer and a traders of his stock is by definition a risk taker. It is very essential to acquaint the entrepreneur with the characteristics of the risk factors, its consequences and the management strategies. It is only, if the trader has through awareness of risk factor he can take the sting out his vulnerability.

Understanding the logistics of the Risk we may arrive at a useful definition in business perspective. *Risk is the likelihood of significant damage in profit resulting from persuing a particular business approach after duly analysing the probabilities.* The foregoing text discusses how can this interpretation to risk help a businessman to draw a safe management strategy to avoid or pass through the risk without unpleasant economic consequences. In business synchronised efforts need to be made through evolving suitable time management strategy for product distribution in tune to the rising demand for the product in a given environment. Doing this, will imrpove the chances of taking an objective decision.

Types of Risk

There are two major categories of Risk in business. They are (i) Pure risks and (ii) Entrepreneurial risks. The risk of the latter category is commonly experienced by the producers-cum-traders of marginal, small and medium capital business firms located in the rural and urban areas. The entrepreneurial risk include the factors within the control of business like change in product design, advertisement trends and levels of consumer preference for the product. Such risks can not be guarded against the insurance cover. The pure risk is the situation emerging largely from the natural causes which are uncontrolable. Such risks can be protected by insuring the estimated income from the business or the overall enterprise. The best example that can be cited in this regard is the insurance of the crops against natural calamities.

Let us examine the types of entrepreneurial risks in the business environment. They are:

* introduction of new product or service in the market,
* professional mistake in decision making
* collaborations of firms, merger or take overs
* adoption of new technology and cost escallation
* organisational change, and
* cost suiting experiments to promote the product market.

The new products launched pilotly in the market possess the risk of consumer acceptance in its physical and monitory forms. The professional mistake is often sighted by the entrepreneur in the pre-mature stage of the business when it reaches the break even point. The mistake is largely felt in wrong selection of the product, lack of availability of the service for the product, price structure, distribution planning and the negligence of the existing competitive environment. Such mistakes lead the entrepreneurs to collaborate with other firms stronger than them or takeover the lower turnover firms to revamp the zest of business and profit targets. Sometime, the new marketing technology resulted in brand switching approach, attracts the ambitious entrepreneurs excallating the cost of production ultimately pushing up the prices of the product at the end user.

It is necessary to understand that the risk element in business is not always obvious as it is related with the end user of the product or services. It emerges as an emotional reaction than an objective approach to revive the opportunity cost that has lost. However, in the entrepreneurial firms growing in the rural and urban areas many risk situations are created by the lack of technical, professional and management skills.

Measuring the Risk

By and large risk is a behavioural factor. Though it can be measured in terms of money, considerable human factor is involved in the form of 'hunch'. It carries considerable value when combined with the statistical values. Theoretically, the following techniques are used to analyse the risk in business:

* standard deviation analysis
* probability
* simulation and model building
* liner programming
* queuing theory
* exponential forecasting and
* decision free analysis

However, the real life situation is somewhat different. The collective decisions and logistics on the qualitative parametres often lead to prolific results to avoid risk in business. More reliable method of risk assessment involve the use of judgment and the combined wisdom of experienced people — taking full account of the available information. This method is known as 'Brainstorming' which make use of accumulated wisdom and experience of a homogeneous group of people. This method explore:

* what can go wrong in the business?
* How will the market react to the strategy and
* what will be the reaction of the end users on the product?

It is essential that the problems to be solved must be clearly stated and understood before any sensible decision can be made using the judgment based techniques alike the discussed 'Brainstorming' method. The insurance companies which are most concerned with the risk assessment largely depend on the judgment based techniques on the qualitative parametres.

Future Threats

Conceptually marketing is a function of demand and supply, for the products produced in a given space and time. It has different area specific, product specific and socio-cultural characteristics, which determine the product's standing in the market. These factors, by and large govern the trade practice in the markets held in a particular region. However, this may change time and again according to the buyer's and seller's perception towards the marketing efficiency. The rural entrepreneurs, who are the basic suppliers of raw materials to some of the farm and non-farm industries, largely transact in rural markets with small quantities of marketable surplus. They could earn a small margin of profit which covers their subsistance needs. Such economic conditions, limit the extent of capital investment though it may be potentially profitable to invest more. However, at the same time the business ventures are more risky. This is one of the consequences of the area specific characteristic of the market. Likewise, product specific market conditions reflect highly favourable opportunities for maximum sales realisation when the buyers are elite and the sellers have more prolific ways of communicating the product. Besides, the branding and packaging of the product is also important in marketing and this can be popularised through the communication approaches. In modern marketing system, the Approachability, Accessibility, and Adaptability constitute the core strategy for product marketing.

The 3A's determine efficiency of product marketing, irrespective of area specifications — rural or urban. The urban markets, largely in private and corporate sectors have been fast developing ever since the marketing communication devises emerged in the trade-world. Apart from strong communication approaches, the product markets are capital oriented and can withstand short run and casual market risks. The use of selling method by price mechanism has been another important aspect of penetrating the products into the competitive markets. The urban markets, with such, manifold characteristics, which are organised to a large extent impos ` social and economic threats to the rural unorganised markets. Of these, the major threat is of the product saleability in urban market environment. The threats to the rural product markets are also their viability and sustainability. The Table 6.1 exhibits the broad areas of threats to rural markets and concerned issues that effect thereby.

The rural markets are conventional and in developing economic conditions, which concentrated around marketing and product movement, face many threats. In fact a rural market is an assortment of different variables within the subsistence economic system from the point of view of grower-seller. They are not capital oriented and unable to shift their product designs at par with the urban markets.

Table 6.1: Broad Areas of Market Threats with Reference to Rural Products

Areas of Market Threat			
Psycho-Social	*Product*	*Marketing*	*Economic*
– Inclination towards popular brands	– Non-conventional	– Dumping effect	– Low Profit
– Three A's consideration	– Mechanical – Financing of products	– Branding & – Packaging	– Sustainability
– Higher Consumer Awareness	– New Design & Durability	– Pricing techniques	– Unprotected market
– Impact of advertisement	– Limited resources	– Systematic product distribution	
	– Lack of skills & entrepreneurship	– Well knitted – operation strategy	

In fact the fashion advertisement (FAds) have the dominant role in stimulating buyers' perceptions and selling their brand in competitive markets. Such stimulies are of short span and create a lot of demand shifts in the product market. The rural markets, thus may have a greater threat of FAds in selling their products even in their hinterland. It is an effective instrument in creating consumer awareness.

Impact of FAds

In management terms the fashion advertisements are called FAds. Advertisement is an effective tool of communication, particularly in rendering the market awareness. Advertising a product, helps to mobilise the information on its utility and adoptability among the consumers. The impact on buyer's perception for the advertised product is deep rooted and develops inclination towards the same. However the intensity of the buyers' inclination depends upon the frequency of communication and the type of media. It is observed that the impression on product buying lasts long if the communication is brought out in periodic intervals. The impact of short-run advertisement may be seen, provided the communication is withdrawn in short time with high frequency. Thus for an effective and long run business plan, the advertisements of products should be representative and periodical. The short-run impacts are noticed in the situation of changing fashion or buyers' perceptions towards a product. There are some products particularly conspicuous ones, which attract a particular segment of consumers in short announcement, like, textiles, automobiles etc. which are absolutely fashion prone. Such products' sales realisation will be more for a short while and recede quickly. However, there are other products which need periodical announcement to withstand the market competition and keep intact the consumer's taste. The products of regular use like washing powders, soaps, food products etc. for which there is a neck to neck competition, an effective and frequent communication network is required. By and large such characteristics are noticed among the products of private sector. In rural areas the product communication system is weak due to many reasons. Firstly the communication skill and approach is lagging among rural products and sellers. Secondly, there are financial constraints for issuing frequent advertisements in the market. Finally, the product produced in rural areas are of traditional nature and need perceptional changes among buyers which is a difficult task. It needs storming communication system, as the rural industries product are much unaware of such measures.

The FAds coming from private and corporate sectors have considerable influencing background. To assist in reviewing this background and placing the product in market, there are two acronyms : PEST and SWOT. The initial letters for PEST represent four areas with direct implications on product, area and clientele. They are political, economical, sociological and technological background for influencing through FAds. The political decisions have immediate business implications. The economic and sociological aspects, of course, overlap with the political decisions. However, the FAds backed with technological merits of the product have larger acceptability among consumers as compared to the other backgrounds.

SWOT is another well known marketing analysis which has equal application on advertisement and its impact on the clientele. The analysis is made, bearing in mind many factors with reference to PEST and likely future trends. The FAds present, strength of their product, weaknesses of the competing products, opportunities for product advancement, and threats facing in absence of their proposed products viz. threats may be economical, personal, health etc. Thus the SWOT analysis in FAds stands for strength, weakness, opportunity and threats. The FAds extensively and intensively use these two backgrounds for making the marketing communication more effective and acceptable. Such methods are not adopted by the rural entrepreneurs to sell their product. It is one of the reasons, they are facing the market threat from the private and corporate sector.

Market Planning

Marketing in rural areas is a complex phenomenon. It has a greater bias towards the social and behavioural aspects rather than business economics. The various factors affecting the dimension of rural marketing have been discussed in the pretext. An effective marketing system is one of the major determinants for generating better income levels in rural areas. Since of the entrepreneurs are also sellers of their products in rural markets, an improved market conditions will have a direct bearing on their income level and so also on the socio-economic conditions.

The product-market planning need to be done in a phased manner. Initially an extensive survey of available infrastructure, commodities produced, consumer behaviour towards the existing products, technology, resource and product distribution pattern would be a helpful tool of device an appropriate marketing system. In improving the marketing conditions of REFs, state has to play an important role till they overcome the organisational and financial conflicts of embryonic stage. However, in this process it is expected that the role of state should be sympathetic towards the entrepreneur's marketing economy but need not to make it dependent on state. This may lead to many behavioural problems in long run from the entrepreneurs point of view. The first and foremost requirement in planning product marketing system in rural areas is to develop a non-conventional technology for product marketing. This may be developed in the areas of product packaging, branding, market communication through FAds, and distribution planning.

The State patronage is necessary for the break through of such technology in rural areas. However, the most important aspect that has to be kept in view is the accessibility, approachability and adoptability of the technology in rural entrepreneurial conditions. In this regard, there is a need for generating extensive social awareness and attitude towards development in a competitive economy.

Behavioural Dimensions in Change Management

The dynamism in the development environment is reflected in demand led planning, participatory designs, administrative responsiveness and effective communication. However, the innovative changes in development practices involve high risk in terms of goal realisation and the social acceptance in the long term. The innovations in the rural development planning which are the change agents constitute reformation of the traditional or existing methods or introduction of the new approaches altogether for delivering the social goods and services in the existing multi-agency organisational network. By and large, implementation of such innovative rural development plans is a complex process, which requires the use of knowledge in order to generate common interest in adoption of an innovative implementation process through the existing administrative set-up. The grass-roots level functionaries being less exposed to the economic development ethic, possess more reluctance towards change in the prevailing practices and thus, may show less significant impact initially on the overall outcome. However, it is essential to evolve an appropriate diffusion process to promote the demand led rural development planning process and the strategies of implementation thereof.

The Behavioural Cycle

The process of innovation in a society passes through various stages and seldom take place at a given spatial framework. However it is participated by the different persons and organisations. The model of innovative development process in a social context is illustrated in Diagram 6.1. The long-run acceptance of such change in rural areas lead to adoption of the change. However to achieve this objective it is essential to have homogeneous diffusion of alternative planning process [APP] in rural areas to create effective development and change.

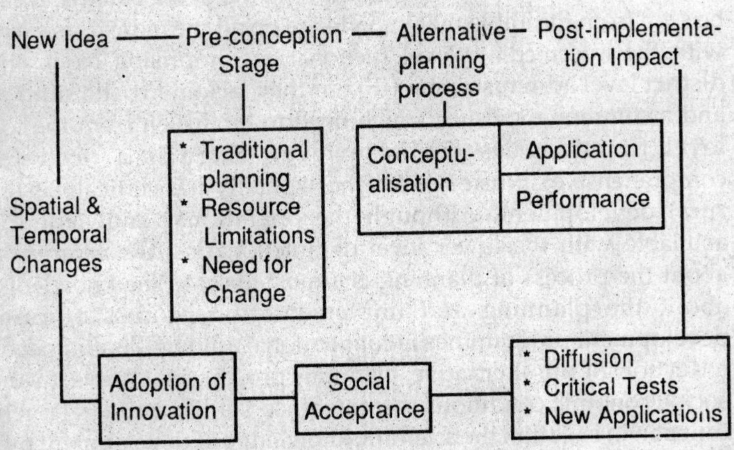

Diagram 6.1: Diffusion and Adoption Cycle

However the theory of diffusion and adoption of APP has to be conceptualised with reference to some assumptions. It may be kept in view while considering the concept of diffusion and adoption of APP for rural development that these issues also possess the linkages with the local demand for employment, income and marketing through the existing development agencies.

1. The beneficaries have low capital, investment, production and marketing finance syndrome which make them more risk averse if the changes in the planning process is made without the social consent,
2. The adoption of APP is largely subject to the effective training at the grass roots level imparted to the functionaries,
3. The experimentation of APP need analytical insight to assess the local demand and

Adoption Analysis

The behavioural dimensions influence the decision making on various functional issues in rural firms to a large extent. The aspects related to knowledge, attitude, and practice [KAP] constitute the core behavioural determinants which have major role in the adoption process of ATs. Table 6.2 exhibits the major knowledge types required for diffusion and adoption of APP in rural development planning to improve the overall status. It can be seen from the Table that knowledge on all the indicators exists with the intermediate level fuctionaries comprising block and district level administration (IF) but they lack in logistic support and a common exposure which need to be driven from the top level functionaries (TF). However, there is a need for comprehensive diffusion of APP horizontally and vertically in the rural development. Although the operational knowledge is available with the lower level of functionaries, the awareness about the process of planning is almost absent. The knowledge about the planning and implementation process of rural development programmes is conventional among LFs and needs induction of an alternative planning process matchable to the socio-economic conditions thereof. Since the LFs and IFs largely function in isolation the scientific knowledge of development mix and its application is also essential after the attitude building towards the adoption of APP.

Table 6.2: Diffusion of Knowledge in Change Adoption Process

	Knowledge Type	*Availability*	*Status*		*Requirement*
			IF	*TF*	
1.	Target oriented planning know-how	LF/IF	CN	IE	APP
2.	Demand led planning	TF	—	IE	CE
3.	Knowledge, attitude and development mix*	IF/TF	IE	LS	CE
4.	Innovation management	IF	RA	—	APP

LF = Local level functionaries, IF = Intermediate functionaries Block/ Dist, TF = Top level functionaries, IE = Innovative exposure, CN = Conventional, APP= Alternative planning process, CE = Common exposure, LS = Logistic support, RA = Risk averse

*Explains plan formulation, implementation, monitoring and evaluation.

The institutional support is therefore, a pre-requisit for the adoption of the APP in rural development optimum results. The planning process know-how not only refers to technical and managerial skills required for adoption but also need the understanding on the demand led perspectives of development in rural areas. The penetration of the knowledge on the above issues will synthesise the KAP behaviour and its magnitude in the rural development administration in the vertical or horizontal direction.

The vertical diffusion order (VDO) refers to the diffusion of APP approach in all the levels of functionaries in ascending order e.g. TF—IF—LF. The diffusion of APP approach follows similar path in horizontal diffusion order (HDO) while the intra regional diffusion in rural areas e. g. Village 1——Village 2——Village 3. The local level functionaries and the beneficiaries of rural development programme play catalytic role in HDO for alternative planning.

The available knowledge, requirements and the gap therein develop further components 'attitude' and 'practice' towards adoption of diffused technology. The development of attitude is a process which includes many goal oriented perceptions on the production and marketing technology over a period of time. The motivational factors in developing the attitude and practice to lead a phenomenal change may be termed a 'drive' stands significantly in this context. The Diagram 6.2 exhibits the association

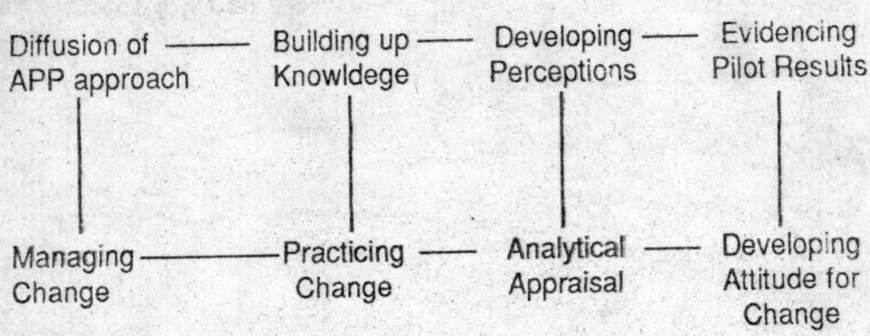

Diagrarn 6.2: Syncronised Stages in Change Management

between the attitude and practice in technology extension. It is a process and faces many social and economic interventions. The traditional and cultural patterns, lack of economic efficiency, lack of achievement motivation, external locus of market control and a sub-culture of poverty have over ridden the development concerns to accept the change in practice in rural areas. Thus there is a need for developing more concern towards the alternative planning process at the local level functionaries to generate logistic development base at the grass roots.

7

The Challenge

In the post-independence period considerable thinking has been laid by the Indian planners in developing the rural areas by giving substantial emphasis on promoting the social and economic status of rural people. The need for overall development in rural areas has been stressed in Indian planning all through the years. The era of village development started with the Second Five Year Plan which emphasised the implementation of various community development projects in different sectors through the Panchayat Raj Institution (PRIs). Later in 1969, government formulated schemes with direct intervention to assist the rural poor. In the subsequent years many programmes and schemes have been designed and floated in rural areas assessing the local needs and programme objectives at micro level. The basic thesis after these development inputs in Indian planning has been to achieve better economic growth with social justice. Many of these development programmes have undergone considerable changes in implementation process observing set backs at different levels of functionaries. In late seventies, reviewing the efforts made to uplift the rural economy through various development programmes in successive Five Year Plans, the policy on rural development has largely stressed on achieving the sustainable development within the broad objectives. Therefore, considerable efforts have been put towards sectoral development with decentralised approaches.

Administrative Network

The administrative process in rural development moves around the district administration which provides the basic operational machinery. It is in practice since 1781 when the district became the nuclie of the revenue collection from the village clusters spread over a demarcated region and the 'locus standie' of collector had been the supreme in the district.

However the arrangement undergone subsequent changes with the introduction of departmental network and hierarchical integration. The collector has been defined as the focuie of the administrative network in the district and has to coordinate horizontally with various departments involved in achieving the development objectives of the district. After the departmental lines we.e vertically organised, the responsibility of their sychronisation and coordination, vested with the district head being the main channel of communication for policy matters between the state and the district. Thereby, with the set up of administrative departments, the tasks have become specific and proper matching of activities in the implementation process has become essential for optimising operational efficiency in general. However, in particular, the existing administrative infrastructure in blocks for executing rural development programmes has been diversified to a large extent by involvement of numerous department in block administration. This has caused improper coordination, though block administration is the main agency for executing a large number of schemes introduced by various departments. Besides institutional coordination there are many other problems like selection of scheme, implementation approach and bureacratisation, which attributed to the problem of inter-departmental linkages.

The introduction of Integrated Rural Development Programme in 1980-81 has thrown a new concept of inter-institutional linkages, which has infact an important tool for achieving the objectives of economic development in rural areas. This programme has put-forth the challenge for input supply, finance, technological support, output marketing and monitoring among different institutions. The task ahead was to establish linkages at various levels of operations in time with different institutions like district administration, banks, marketing agencies, engineering departments etc to streamline the process of development.

The existing structure of multi-agency approach while in operation showed some innate constraints. The absence of clear demarcation of operational boundaries, tasks, clear role perception, etc. brought considerable strain in activating the process. Besides these lacunae the dual control system of institutional head and administration heads at various levels was found to be one of the constraints in developing mutual coordination among various institutes for functional efficiency. The local political interference, time and again, has showed another obstruction in carrying out the functional linkages effectively to the field. The diagram 1.6 exhibits the order of inter-institutional linkages required for an effective implementation of rural development programmes at gross-roots level.

The chain of institutional linkages start from village level workers (VLW) and block development officers (BDO) who identify the beneficiary and appropriate scheme to his socio-economic attitude and later on acceptance of the proposal by financing institution, it is further processed at District Rural Development Agency (DRDA) at the district level for consideration of government subsidy. The Diagram 1.6 clearly exhibits the issues of interdisciplinary management at various levels. An approach to credit institution through BDO and DRDA forms the first order linkage while technology, entrepreneurship development programmes (EDP), marketing and monitoring activities constitute the second order linkage. The evaluation of the economic benefits of the programme and formulation of alternative strategies may be defined as third order linkages which are policy oriented and dealt by the controlling authority.

Responsiveness

Administrative responsiveness to the implementation process of rural development programmes is one of the major considerations for effective commissioning of the programme or scheme thereof. By and large it is a process of inter and intra-departmental coordination at various levels. The basic requirement is the coordination between two economic segments of production and marketing. The process of implementation of various development programmes in rural areas throughout the five year plans have been experienced that most of them are production oriented. Thus in the operational process of the programme, the concept of marketing is over looked though it is one of the important forward linkages for production promotion, income generation and overall economic growth of the sector. Therefore, the greater economic crisis has been often emphasised for market responsiveness of rural products. In this regard, there is a need for, greater concentration on state protection at embryonic stage of rural industries, technology transfer and development of infrastructure. However, in agriculture sector regulating the trade in village markets need to be given due importance.

In early eighties with the introduction of IRDP for multi-sectoral rural development, a number of measures were taken to evolve a balanced implementation approach through establishing inter-linkages with financial, technical, extension and other operational resources. The directly productive rural development programmes had to some extent shown favourable economic impact on the target group. However because of the inherent problem of effective coordination among the departments carrying the responsibilities of ensuring input supply, output marketing, extension and administration, the implementation of integrated rural development programme has shown regional variation in marking overall efficiency. Added to this, the problem of inadequate extension staff and lack of proper work assignment with time limit and the priorities at the village level are also the issues for consideration at various levels, more critically.

Government has shouldered the major responsibility of face-lifting the rural economy in the post-independence planning era. There were numerous rural development programmes drafted and implemented in preceding five year plans. By and large, at the end of Fifth Five Year Plan, the Integrated Rural Development Programme (IRDP) emerged as a filtered policy out of the past experiences. Many of the rural development programmes were merged into IRDP and has been launched in all the blocks of the country in 1981 as a major attempt on poverty alleviation. The objectives of the programme has been largely motivated by the thinking that the rural poverty is a consequence of low productivity due to lack of finance, assets and appropriate skills. Influenced with such parameters IRDP has been sought to provide a package of assistance by way of institutional credit and subsidy to augment the productivity and income of rural households lying below poverty line. In the Seventh Five Year Plan the physical achievement of IRDP in terms of families assisted was 115 per cent over the set target of 160.37 lakh. The IRDP has set encouraging results in the Goa state. The achievement of objectives of IRDP vested in bringing the poorest of the poor above poverty line has been well achieved. In all 74.2

per cent families have crossed the poverty line in the country during 1989-90. However the IRDP/DWCRA programmes as such lack in adequate backward and forward linkages (B&FL) which is instrumental in incremental income. By and large marketing is one of the areas that has great significance in providing enhanced scope for the betterment of IRDP beneficiaries.

The existing structure of multi-agency approach while in operation had some innate constraints. The absence of clear demarcation of operational boundaries, tasks, clear role perception, etc. brought considerable strain in activating the process. Besides these lacunae, the dual control system of institutional head and administration head at various levels was found to be one of the constraints in developing mutual co-ordination among various institutes for achieving functional efficiency. The local political interference, time and again, has showed another obstruction in carrying out the functional linkages effectively to the field.

The chain of institutional linkages start from village level workers (VLW) or Gram Sevikas and block development officers (BDO) who identify the beneficiary and scheme appropriate to his socio-economic attitude and later on acceptance of the proposal by financing institution, it is further processed at Rural Development Agency (RDA) for consideration of government subsidy. An approach to credit institution through BDO and DRDA forms the first order linkage while technology, entrepreneurs development programmes (EDP), marketing and monitoring activities constitute the second order linkage. The evaluation of the economic benefits of the programme and formulation of alternative strategies may be defined as third order linkages which are policy oriented and dealt by the controlling authority.

Administrative responsiveness to the implementation process of rural development programmes is one of the major considerations for effective commissioning of the programme or scheme thereof. By and large it is a process of inter and intra-departmental coordination at various levels. The basic requirement is the co-ordination between two economic segments of production and marketing. The process of implementatior of various development programmes in rural areas throughout the

Five Year Plans have been experienced that most of them are production oriented. Thus in the operational process of the programme, the concept of marketing is over looked though it is one of the important forward linkages for production promotion, income generation and overall economic growth of the sector. Therefore, the greater economic crisis has been often emphasised for market responsiveness of rural products. In this regard, there is a need for, greater concentration on state protection at embryonic stage of rural industries, technology transfer and development of infrastructure. However, in agriculture sector, regulating the trade in village markets need to be given due importance.

Looking at the various issues on coordination, product-market segmentation, consumer behaviour, marketing approaches and B&FL, the present study has some significant recommendations emerging out of analysis.

Administering Market Horizons

The marketing of rural products either rural to rural or rural to urban in developing countries like India is being performed under uncontrolled conditions and do not possess any organised functioning pattern. The status of rural marketing has been explained in the discussion of previous theme, which dealt with various economic and operational gaps thereof. Thus, appropriate planning for rural products marketing in terms of trade channels, infrastructure, technology and behavioural dimensions need to be emphasised for achieving better economic efficiency. However prior to discussing in depth the planning process of rural products marketing, it is essential to identify the existing gaps in the system. The product marketing in rural areas have various conflicts at primary and secondary levels.

The primary level conflicts in marketing of rural products are related with the characteristics of economic environment and production. The lack of effective coordination at local level with the available resources, production process and the outlets is often found responsible for unfavourable interactions of market forces. The following factors attribute to such conditions at primary level:

(i) mis-match of consumer demand and product characteristics;
(ii) lack of quality and innovative concept;

(iii) absence of product recognition, packaging, branding and consumer awareness;

(iv) in adequate raw material, infrastructure, product promotional prospects;

(v) competitive threat, higher dependency on private trade channel and lack of adequate institutional arrangements for production and marketing support.

Besides, the rural products are not competitive market oriented and they are sold in isolation. The products of their REFs commonly emerge as a by product of their main occupation. As such, most of the products of REFs do not aptly match with the consumer demand and quality. It is one of the reasons, that REFs largely depend on the private traders who procure these products at comparably low price and market in dense transaction places taking higher degree of risk. Since the REFs do not have any choice of channel in absence of trade alternatives like cooperatives, the dependency on private trade channel is seen high. The innovative characteristic is also lacking in rural products as they use conventional techniques of production and face the threat of contemporary products with better quality and designs in the market. Besides, there is no constant watch on the market trend by REFs to assess the existing demand and consumer perceptions towards the products. Many market research studies have shown that the lack of proper product exposure to the market and potential consumers has the major obstruction the product mobility from rural to urban areas. The diagram 7.1 exhibits the cause and effect of various factors related with production and marketing economy of REFs.

The two analytical segments of rural marketing system cause and effect have inter and intra-factor associations. The cause of low production is associated with the low degree of technology adoption and weak resources of marketing finance. Similarly the characteristics of unorganised rural product market is largely an attribution of feeble infrastructure and marketing communication structure. The effects of these causes will be traders' lobby, lack of consumer awareness about the product and risk to a large extent. However, lack of proper network of product distribution, limited scope of market expansion and isolation of consumer are also the adverse effects of the existing rural marketing system. Thus, there is a need to evolve an effective marketing mix in context to rural products considering the social and economic environment.

Diagram 7.1: Gaps in Rural Marketing System

Cause	*Effect*
Low Production	Poor Perception
	Risk
Conventional Marketing	Low Demand
Technology	Growth of Substitutes
Unorganised Marketing	Traders Lobby
Market Finance	Low Investment
	Limited Scope
Infrastructure	Poor Distribution
	Network
	Poor Accessibility
Market Communication	Low Consumer Awareness
	Isolation

Social Acceptance

The product recognition with reference to indigenous rural products in market has becoming an increasingly important element in product promotion. The social acceptance of the product is a behavioural stigma which decides the basic trade options whether to mobilise a particular product in consumer clique or to drop out. Since a group of potential consumers or traders constitute the nuclie of the business. The consensus on the quality, branding, distribution pattern, pricing and other comparative advantageous over the similar products form the level of social acceptance of the product.

It has been observed in some rural marketing studies, that the rural products do not acquire considerable acceptance in the society due to their product characteristics to a large extent. However, the aesthatic value may exists in them but ranks less in consumers' priority from the point of optimum usage. Besides, dynamic markets commonly accept innovatory products and draw more attraction of buyers. The lack of contemporary designing and style of product presentation in the market are another important aspects which determine the overall product recognition. There are short run and long run product recognition concepts in the markets, which are largely governed by the conceived perceptions, attitude and behaviour of the prevailing and existing buyers. Table 7.1 exhibits behavioural dimension of product recognition at different social hierarchies. The characteristics depicted in the Table explain that the product recognition at the lower stratum of society takes into consideration the price and quantitative aspects of the product in short and long run. The innovation in prevailing products or series of products with attractive fashion advertisements and special bargain offers are the parameters to accept the products for short run by the consumers of middle stratum of the society. However, in the long run the quality differentiation durability, disposability and value component and other common advantageous over the similar products are the parameters which guide the consumer's decision. There are different dimensions for accepting the product at the high stratum of the society. The price factor affects less the buying decisions at this level. The factors related to conspicuous taste, asthetic value, market presentation and durability account at higher levels of society.

Table 7.1: Behavioural Dimensions of Product Recognition in Social Hierarchy

Levels of Society	*Behavioural Structure*	
	Short run	*Long run*
Lower	Quantitative considerations, low price, easy accessibility, substantial supply, instant consumption.	Quantitative and monetary gains over other competitive products
Middle	Innovative, change in packaging, buying incentives, consumable, attractive FAds, impulsive bargain.	Quality differentiation, durability, resale value additional gains over existing products.
High	Conspicuous taste, impressive FAds, easy in handling, easily accessible.	Asthetic value, durability status mark, resale value rennovable.

The product recognition is a complex process and to some extent inconsistent too as it shifts frequently along with the social and behavioural environment. The rural products thus, have less opportunities to make deep penetration to change the perception and attitudes of buyers. The urban traders often procure this business psychology and procure raw material from rural markets to introduce the products in tune to the attitude of potential consumers.

Market Planning

The product policy should never be considered in isolation. It should always be planned in relation to market. There are two types of products — (i) existing and (ii) potential, likewise there are two groups of consumers — (i) prevailing and (ii) potential. The product plan has to match with the product - consumer groups for efficient results. The product market plan can have three directions as under :

(i) New consumers with existing products;
(ii) New products with existing consumers; and
(iii) New products with new consumers.

It would be easy to plan for a product market in above product-consumer - mix. Any of these segments would be a cost effective proposition for planning and an appropriate mix to achieve business target. In product planning, the analysis of product acceptability is most important aspect and a careful decision need to be taken in this regard. The analysis has to be done keeping the scope of product saleability and profitability in view while making the decision on the product - consumer mix. However the substitution effect of the competing product also need to be taken care of while planning for a product in a market. The product positioning is the next stage of the product planning which need to be assessed by the parameters of demand concentration, accessibility, approachability and infrastructure. The product can be positioned in such markets where the demand concentration is high without any risk. The product markets can be classified as high concentration (HC) and low concentration (LC) segments with regard to a particular product or a group of products. The viability of the product plan for marketing need to appraised properly before implementing the plan or introducing the product in the market. The appraisal would facilitate to test the feasibility of plan whether the product would fetch considerable sales or not. The detail plan for marketing can be formulated based on the positive results of plan appraisal.

An appropriate pricing policy has a positive impact on profit making and sales realisation. The pricing is a directly related factor to the profit and sale of products under different market conditions. The pricing policy adopted will reflect the positioning of the product in the market. These issues be viewed as either high-price or low-price policies. The effective pricing strategies may be considered according to product age in the market - embryonic, mature and aging.

There are three basic elements : (i) product recognition, (ii) price structure and (iii) the distribution planning which are required to develop an effective marketing mix. The relative importance of these three elements varies from product to product and from time to time. Distribution, is often the key to a successful sales and marketing policy. The objective of distribution planning is to make the product available to the consumers at a more convenient outlet. The distribution planning for products should be considered with prime importance to withstand the market competition. It is because, if a competitive product is available at approachable outlets or at low price, there are all chances of foregoing the sale. Therefore, to deal under such competitive market situation a systematic planning for delivering the product to the consumers through different distribution channels, need to be determined. The time and distance factor for the delivery of goods normally influences the buying decisions where the manufacturing of products are subject to consumer order, occasional demands and door to door delivery promises. In this regard the planning need to be done evolving different methods for efficient product distribution through identified channels. In this process, there is a need to look into the infrastructural factors viz. transport, road, communication etc in support of the channel efficiency. In fact the consumer is only interested in getting the product but a lot of responsibility lies with the marketing personnel in delivering the product at appropriate time and place.

The distribution planning may invariably be based on the

market survey carried out at the time of preparing the business plan. The distribution planning should be to make the products available to the larger number of consumers at lower marketing costs. To reduce the cost of marketing it is required to determine the most feasible channel. The product characteristics and the operational area are the major factors to be considered while selecting a distribution channel. In any channel different distribution approach can be adopted to get the products more economically to the ultimate user. The important factor to be assessed in this process is the cost effectiveness. It is observed that, longer the chain of intermediaries in product distribution, higher is the cost of marketing. Since cost is one of the determinants of profit, it should also be viewed from the angle of product distribution. The exclusive distribution approach is always confined to an area. Such distribution plan can be useful in the areas (i) where the demand concentration for the product is low (ii) which are located at distance from the high concentration areas i. e. urban places (iii) the storage, transportation and other overhead costs are higher and (iv) the competition is absent or very low. In urban areas where market competition for the product is high and the retailing is at large scale, selective distribution policy would be more useful. However, the approach of extensive distribution of products is regarded by retailers and consumers in rural areas and in the location where the purchasing power of consumers is low but a large number of retailers are in business fray. In other words, such approach would help the market condition where the turnover of business is relatively small. By and large the following seven factors should be considered while forming the product distribution policy.

i. The product - characteristics and consumer recognition.
ii. Size and value of sales - extent of sales realisation.
iii. Market area - consumer coverage, retailers and other traders.
iv. Existing methods of distribution - impact, lopesides.
v. Needed efforts - consumer approachability, appealing to distributors, cost effective and sales realisation.
vi. Overhead costs - operational expenses, personnel management, and,
vii. Monitoring - channelising distribution, cash flow, payments.

These factors are inter-related and affect the whole network of product distribution. The distribution chain or network may be long or wide, there is a need for effective control without which the entire business plan may break mid-way. Marketing of products in a competitive environment has many ways. The FADs and strategies building for optimum sales realisation are prominent among them. As discussed earlier, the FAds have greater impact on the elite clienatele group as compared to other measure used for raising up the sales. The product branding and packaging technology is the core input for FAds. Attractive packaging and popular branding have significant role in market expansion and product promotion. In competitive market economy the brands are hired by the manufactures, for product marketing. In this system, the product is manufactured by the small scale units or to some extent by REFs. In marketing such products manufacturer gets fringe benefits while the brand owner gets higher share in consumer's rupee. As such, these firms (REFs) may not be in a position to establish their own brand due to many weakness pertaining to capital, technical know-how and market guidance. The future threat in this regard can be visualised in the light of REFs autonomy, in selling their product. In long run, the REFs identity will be only as a manufacturing unit but not as a product seller.

Packaging in the competitive product market is an important determinant as for as the buyer's behaviour is concerned. More attractive and durable is the packaging of any product, greater would be the product resistance and market demand. 'The New packs' may be the hard-core of some FAds which could be more appealing to the target customers. It requires enough capital to invest in packaging technology. The REFs do not afford to meet such high capital requirement and hence the products are traditionally packed.

The expansion of product market largely depends on the way the product sales is organised. The REFs, have limited operational area as the entrepreneurs largely depend on floor sales in local markets. There are many techniques adopted in organising effective sales. They are, departmental stores, super markets, mobile sale units, emporium, exhibitions and fun sales. Among these systems, the departmental stores and supermarkets have received considerable attention in towns, urban and semi-urban areas while the mobile shops and fun sales have been induced the buyers in rural areas. The fun sales is organised in less developed areas through the folk entertainment programme. Such system is being observed in different Asian countries. In future more flexible methods of sales, may appear to cover larger number of customers and larger area under product market. The REFs need to require some of these sales organisation methods to stand at par with the large business firms. The threat remains, otherwise in future too.

Select References

Abbot J.C: Role of Marketing in Development of Backward Agricultural Economics, *Journal of Farm Economics*, 44, 1962, pp.349-62.

Anderson M Patrica: Marketing Communication, Prentice - Hall, Englewood Cliffs, New Jersey, 1986.

Bhaduri A: Agricultural Backwardness and Semi-feudalism, *Economic Journal*, 83, 1973.

Comment: Cultural Values in India's Economic Development, *Annales of American Academy of Political and Social Sciences*, No. 305, 1956, pp. 81-91.

George P.T., Mohanan N. and Rajagopal, Status Paper on Co-operative Movement in India, National Institute of Rural Development, Hyderabad, 1985.

Government of India: Draft Sixth Five Year Plan, Planning Commission, 1980 - 85.

Government of India: Report of the Working Group on Rural Roads, National Transport Policy Committee, Planning Commission, 1979, pp.49-51.

Government of India: Draft Seventh Five Year Plan, Part II, Planning Commission, p.56.

Government of India: Draft of the Scheme on DSMS, Department of Rural Development, New Delhi, 1991.

Government of Goa: Rural Development Statistics, 1989-91.

GHRSSIDC: Brief note on functional and organisational pattern of Goa Handicrafts Small Scale Industries Development Corporation, Panaji 1991.

Gupta V.K. and Gaikwad V.R., Guide to Management of Small Farmer's Co-operatives, FAO, Rome.

Hyder Goran: Approaches to Corporative Development: Blue Print VS Green House Approach, in Atterwood DW & Baviskar BS (Eds): Cooperatives and Rural Development. Oxford Delhi, 1987.

Indian Society of Agricultural Economics: Reporteurs Report, 46th Annual Conference, *Indian Journal of Agricultural Economics*, 42(1), 1987, pp.32-33.

Jeffery James B: The Distribution of Consumer Goods, Cambridge University Press, London, 1950, p.14.

Kakwani N & Subarao K: Rural Poverty and its Aleviation in India, *Economic and Political Weekly*, March 31, 1990, pp. 4-12.

Kulkarni K R: Agricultural Marketing in India, Somaiya Publications, Bombay, 1956.

Lauth James H: Economic Consideration in Price Making and Price Structure, *American Journal of Agricultural Economics*, 51(2), 1969, pp.1466-70.

Liang PPE: Market Accessibility and Agricultural Development in Pre-war China, Economic Development and Cultural Change, 309(1), 1981.

McCallend and David C: Power: The Inner Experience, Irvington Publishers, New York, Chap. IV 1975.

Mc Mannan et. ad.: Sales Negotiation Strategies, AMACON, New York, 1977.

NABARD: Potential Linked Credit Plan for North Goa District, 1990-91.

National Institute of Rural Development: Proceedings of the Workshop on DSMA, July 22 -24, 1991.

Oryn R. Young: Formal Theories of Negotiation, University of Illinois Press, Urbana, USA, 1975, p. 408.

Rajagopal: Micro-level Planning for Agricultural Marketing, Renaissance, Delhi, 1988.

Rajagopal: Agri-business and Entrepreneurship, Anmol, New Delhi, 1990.

Rajagopal: Planning and Management of Rural Marketing NIRD, Hyderabad, 1990.

Rajagopal, Dynamics of Agricultural Marketing in Tribal India, Rainbow Publications, Coimbatore, 1986, pp. 37-59.

Rajagopal, Economic Efficiency of Paddy Marketing System in Madhya Pradesh, *Indian Journal of Agricultural Economics*, 41 (4), October-December 1986, pp.583-590.

Rajagopal: An Economic Analysis of Weekly Markets of Bastar Distt. of MP, Ph.D Thesis, Ravishankar University, Raipur, 1984.

Rajagopal: Marketing Linkages in IRDP Lesson from states, Kurukshetra, April 1991.

Rajagopal: Planning and Management of Rural Marketing, Report, National Institute of Rural Development, Hyderabad, 1990.

Rajagopal: Rural Marketing: Gulf Between Policy and Practice, *Financial Express*, January 6, 1992.

Rajagopal: Retailing of Rural Products, : A Goan Experience, *Kurukshetra*, May, 1992.

Rajagopal: Marketing Support for Rural Development Programmes, Reference Document, pp. 1-127, IRMA Anand 1992.

Rajagopal: Rural Marketing in India, Rennaissance Publishing House, New Delhi, 1989.

Rajagopal: Managing Rural Business: Quest For Approach, *Economic Times*, April, 23, 1992.

Rajagopal: Organising Rural Business, Sage, New Delhi, 1994

Ray Amal and Vanitha Subbaiah: Studies on Rural Development Administration in India, World Press, Calcutta, 1988.

Rural Development Agency: Annual Reports, official documents related to IRDP, TRYSEM and DWCRA in North Goa District.

Sikka B K and Vaidya C S: Economics of Production and Marketing of Himachal Apples, *Indian Journal of Agricultural Marketing*, January - June, 1987.

Smith Henery: Retail Distribution: A Critical Analysis, Oxford University Press, London, 1948, pp 12-14.

Sundaram R M: Development Economics — A Framework for Analysis and Policy, John Wiley and Sons, New York 1983, pp. 118-136.

Swaminathan Madhura, For details see village level implementation of IRDP — A comparison between West Bengal and Tamil Nadu, *Economic and Political Weekly*, March 31, 1990, pp. 417-427.

Index